new

Italian Classics in ONE POT

Anna Teresa Callen

A John Boswell Associates/King Hill Productions Book

HarperCollins*Publishers*

HarperCollins books may be purchased for educational, business, or sales promotional use. For information please write: Special Markets Department, HarperCollins Publishers, Inc., 10 East 53rd Street, New York, NY 10022.

FIRST EDITION

Interior design by Stephanie Tevonian
Cover design by Suzanne Noli
Illustrations by John Jinks

Library of Congress Cataloging-in-Publication Data

Callen, Anna Teresa.
    Italian classics in one pot / Anna Teresa Callen.
        p.   cm.
    "A John Boswell Associates/King Hill Productions book."
    Includes index.
    ISBN 0-06-017318-1
    1. Entrées (Cookery)   2. Cookery, Italian.   I. Title.
TX740.C22   1996   96-26201
641.5945—dc20

97 98 99 00 01 HC 10 9 8 7 6 5 4 3 2 1

In memory of the good feasts my mother and father, Raffaella and Giuseppe Vita-Colonna, were able to concoct in a pot for me and my twin brother, Mimmo, when we were growing up.

Contents

Introduction:
Cooking Italian Style

This cookbook contains many recipes that are dear to my heart. For while there is great pleasure in toiling for hours over certain elaborate dishes for special occasions, simple, homey foods like the ones my mother used to make every day have a special place in my memory and in my kitchen today. I know from relatives in my native Abruzzo in the center of Italy, as well as from my own hectic life in New York City, that the demands of our busy lives all over the world make it harder to enjoy the pleasures of cooking, entertaining, and feeding our families. That's why these one-pot Italian dishes are so appealing. The more of the meal that goes into one pot—be it a saucepan, skillet, baking dish, or casserole—the less there is left of the meal to prepare, cook, or clean up.

I plan meals like this often. A little antipasto, or starter, of prosciutto and melon, mozzarella cheese and tomatoes, or lightly dressed grilled vegetables at the beginning; a loaf of crusty Italian bread with the meal; and a selection of cheeses and a basket of fruit or a small sweet at the end are all that's needed to make a delightfully satisfying menu. When friends drop over or the occasion is a special one, my antipasto becomes more elaborate, and the dessert might be an assortment of pastries or a frosted cake.

We Italians, like the Chinese, have a knack for combining ingredients in one pot in an exceptionally tasty way. And most of the time, the preparation is simple and the cooking quick. Let's not forget that Italians are traditionally a frugal people, who often had to do much with little. Vegetables and pasta, that modern American favorite, have long formed the basis of the Mediterranean diet. When there was only a little meat in the house, or perhaps a bit of expensive seafood, it was economical and easy to stretch the meal by throwing some beans or rice into the pot. Now we know how smart that is nutritionally as well.

Food cooked in one pot is also comforting and tends to be appropriate to the seasons: a simple, hearty meat stew chock-full of potatoes and mushrooms in winter; a refreshing pasta dotted with creamy mozzarella and juicy tomatoes bathed in olive oil infused with fragrant basil in summer. What could be more soothing at the first frost of autumn than a warm chicken soup in which plump tortellini swim with bits of meat and chunks of vegetables, or more perfect for that first al fresco lunch of spring than an inventive frittata filled with tender baby vegetables?

Many of the recipes in this book are popular classics. Others are variations on traditional dishes that may be well known in Italy but have not traveled across the ocean. And still others are my more modern interpretations of classic dishes, which add new ingredients to traditional recipes. For we are a nation of individualists. In Italy, even classic dishes vary from town to town as well as from region to region. I, for one, almost never cook a dish the same way twice. I teach cooking, and I always say to my students: "A recipe is like a trampoline. Feel free to jump (that is, to improvise and make substitutions), but don't go overboard and fall off (for example, by putting kiwifruit on a Pizza Napoletana)." There is nothing wrong with being inventive. What counts is the taste and the integrity to original intent.

The cooking techniques used in this book are simple: sautéing, braising, roasting, poaching, and boiling. Some of the preparations cook in a flash; others require a longer, slower cooking time. Either way, no special equipment is needed. All the recipes are tailored to the American kitchen and, for the most part, to ingredients you will find easily in your supermarket.

Whether you choose one of the ingeniously filling Italian soups that make a meal in a bowl, a chicken, your favorite meat, fish or shellfish, pasta, risotto, pizza, or a vegetarian main course, there's an Italian classic here for you. *Buon appetito!*

Soups Like "Mama Mia" Used to Make

Soups, glorious soups—there is no other food more soothing and satisfying than a good *minestra*, as we Italians call soup. On those cold winter nights, I, for one, go straight to the freezer to pull out the last of that lovely soup I made a few weeks ago. I mention the freezer because soups freeze very well, and I always make a point of making enough soup for at least two meals.

In this chapter, most of the *minestre* are quite hefty, since they were planned as meals in themselves. Some are true Italian classics, like the Mixed Bean and Pasta Soup with Ham and Chicken, my version of *pasta e fagioli*, or the rustic, very hearty

Tuscan Minestrone, which is really a *ribollita,* a thick soup that is "reboiled"; others are inspirations and adaptations of old favorites. All you need to round out a meal with one of these soups is a little antipasto, perhaps fresh tomatoes and mozzarella cheese with a drizzling of olive oil and a perfume of basil; a salad with some fennel and cucumber in it; and a dessert that could just be a piece of fruit or a scoop of ice cream.

Artichoke and Rice Soup

My cooking school was the first to give classes on Italian Passover menus. Not being Jewish myself, I invited Jewish colleagues to come and cook. This is based on my friend Elvira Limentani's soup, which comes from the Roman Jewish ghetto. Make this soup with your best homemade chicken broth. Elvira's recipe, with an egg thread garnish, is devised as a light first course. To turn it into a meal, I embellish the soup with artichokes and more eggs, still keeping the authentic flavors. **Makes 6 servings**

8 cups chicken broth
1½ cups converted rice
1 (9-ounce) package frozen
    artichoke hearts, thawed
    and quartered

3 tablespoons fresh lemon juice
3 eggs
Salt
1 tablespoon finely chopped
    parsley

1) In a large flameproof casserole, bring the broth to a boil over high heat. Stir in the rice and reduce the heat to medium. Simmer for 8 minutes. Stir in the artichokes and lemon juice and cook for 5 minutes. The rice will be almost but not quite done.

2) In a small bowl, beat the eggs until well blended. Stirring the broth mixture briskly with a whisk or a fork, slowly pour the egg mixture into the soup. Remove from the heat and season with salt to taste. Serve hot, garnished with parsley.

Mixed Bean and Pasta Soup with Ham and Chicken

T*his is my rendition of pasta e fagioli, the beloved pasta and bean soup.* **Makes 6 to 8 servings**

1 pound mixed dried beans (see above)
2 ham hocks, either fresh or smoked, or 1 large meaty leftover ham bone
¾ teaspoon dried thyme
½ teaspoon dried sage
2 bay leaves
¼ teaspoon freshly ground pepper
1 (28-ounce) can peeled tomatoes, coarsely chopped, juices reserved

3 medium celery ribs, chopped
2 medium onions, chopped
2 medium carrots, chopped
2 garlic cloves, chopped
1 teaspoon salt
12 ounces skinless, boneless chicken breasts, cut into ½-inch cubes
12 ounces smoked ham, cut into ½-inch cubes
¾ cup pastina (tiny soup pasta)
1½ tablespoons chopped fresh parsley

1) In a large soup pot, cover the beans with at least 2 inches of water. Soak 8 to 24 hours. Drain and rinse well.

2) Return the beans to the soup pot. Add 3 quarts water, the ham hocks, thyme, sage, bay leaves, and pepper. Bring to a boil over high heat. Reduce the heat to medium-low, cover, and simmer until the beans are softened but not completely tender, 45 minutes to 1 hour.

3) Add the tomatoes with their liquid, celery, onions, carrots, garlic, and salt. Simmer until the beans are almost tender, 30 to 45 minutes.

4) Add the chicken breast and cook for 5 minutes. Add the smoked ham and pasta and cook until the pasta is tender, about 10 minutes. Remove the ham hocks from the soup and pick out any meat from the bones. Coarsely chop the meat and stir back into the soup, along with the parsley. Discard the bay leaves and serve.

Cabbage and Rice Soup

T*he robust combination of cabbage and pork shows this is a peasant soup, and the presence of rice reveals its northern Italian origin, where rice is grown and is very popular. Even though this is a traditional dish, I use converted rice because it is hard to overcook and will retain its texture even if you reheat the soup.* **Makes 8 servings**

1 tablespoon extra-virgin olive oil
2 ounces thickly sliced prosciutto, finely chopped
2 garlic cloves, minced
1 teaspoon chopped fresh rosemary or ½ teaspoon dried
8 cups shredded red cabbage (about 1½ pounds)
½ cup dry white wine
1 tablespoon balsamic or red wine vinegar
8 cups chicken broth
¾ cup converted rice
12 ounces smoked ham, cut into ½-inch dice
½ cup grated Parmesan cheese

1) In a large soup pot, heat the olive oil over medium heat. Add the prosciutto, garlic, and rosemary. Cook, stirring, until the garlic is fragrant, about 1 minute. Add the red cabbage and stir for 2 minutes. Add 2 tablespoons of the wine. Reduce the heat to low. Cover and cook, adding 2 tablespoons wine every 10 minutes, until the cabbage is very tender, about 30 minutes. Check to be sure the liquid doesn't boil away and add water if needed. Stir in the vinegar.

2) Add the broth to the cabbage and bring to a boil over high heat. Stir in the rice and reduce the heat to medium. Cook until the rice is tender, 15 to 20 minutes.

3) Add the ham and cook just until heated through, about 2 minutes. Ladle into soup bowls, sprinkle the Parmesan cheese on top, and serve.

Carrot and Asparagus Soup
with Tiny Meatballs

This lovely minestra with *pastel colors is perfect for springtime meals. Light, yet full-flavored, it can be a satisfying main course or the elegant first course to an important dinner. Semolina, a golden, coarsely ground durum wheat flour, is available at Italian grocers, natural food stores, and many supermarkets.* ***Makes 6 to 8 servings***

½ pound ground turkey
1 egg, beaten
1½ tablespoons dried bread
  crumbs
1 tablespoon dry marsala wine
½ teaspoon salt
⅛ teaspoon freshly ground
  pepper

1 pound fresh asparagus, tough
  ends removed
6 medium carrots, peeled and
  quartered
1 tablespoon butter
5 cups chicken broth
¼ cup semolina flour
Grated Parmesan cheese

1) In a medium bowl, combine the ground turkey, egg, bread crumbs, marsala, ¼ teaspoon salt, and pepper. Mix to blend well. Using 1 teaspoon for each, form into tiny meatballs and place on a baking sheet. Cover with plastic wrap and refrigerate until ready to use.

2) In a medium soup pot, bring 6 cups of water and the remaining ¼ teaspoon salt to a boil over high heat. Add the asparagus and cook until just tender, 2 to 3 minutes. With tongs transfer the asparagus to a colander and rinse under cold running water until cool; drain. Add the carrots and butter to the asparagus cooking water. Cook until the carrots are completely tender, about 10 minutes. Transfer the carrots and 2 cups of their cooking liquid to a blender and puree.

3) While the carrots are cooking, cut off the asparagus tips and set aside for garnish. Cut the remaining asparagus crosswise into ½-inch lengths.

4) Add the chicken broth to the vegetable cooking liquid remaining in the pot. Bring to a boil; reduce the heat to medium. Quickly but carefully, drop the meatballs one at a time into the broth. Cook at a gentle boil until the meatballs are firm with no trace of pink in the center, 10 to 15 minutes.

5) Stirring constantly, slowly add the semolina. Cook, stirring often, until the soup is thickened, 5 to 10 minutes. Stir in the carrot puree and the sliced asparagus. Cook until heated through, about 2 minutes. If the soup seems too thick, add more broth or water.

6) Ladle into soup bowls and garnish each serving with the reserved asparagus tips. Serve immediately. Pass a bowl of grated Parmesan cheese.

Chicken Soup with Tomatoes, Pasta, and Potatoes

Makes 6 servings

1½ cups small soup pasta, such as tubettini or small shells
3 tablespoons extra-virgin olive oil
1 medium onion, finely chopped
1 pound chicken giblets (hearts and gizzards), coarsely chopped
½ cup chopped fresh basil
2 tablespoons chopped parsley
2 garlic cloves, crushed through a press

3 medium red potatoes (about 12 ounces), peeled and cut into 1-inch cubes
2 bay leaves
2½ pounds ripe plum tomatoes, peeled, seeded, and chopped, or 1 (28-ounce) can peeled tomatoes, chopped, with their juices
Salt and pepper to taste
½ cup grated Parmesan cheese

1) In a large pot of boiling salted water, cook the pasta over high heat until barely al dente, about 8 minutes. Drain the pasta in a colander. Toss with 1 tablespoon of the olive oil and set aside.

2) In the same pot, heat the remaining 2 tablespoons oil over medium heat. Add the onion and cook, stirring often, until the onion is softened and translucent, 3 to 5 minutes. Increase the heat to medium-high. Add the chicken giblets. Cook until lightly browned, about 5 minutes.

3) In a small bowl, mix the basil, parsley, and garlic. Add half of this mixture to the giblets. Cover the remainder with plastic wrap and set aside. Add the potatoes to the pot and cook for 5 minutes. Add 2 cups water and the bay leaves. Bring to a boil, reduce the heat to medium-low, cover, and cook, stirring often, for 10 minutes. Add the tomatoes, salt, and pepper. Continue to cook until the potatoes are tender, 20 to 30 minutes.

4) Stir in the reserved pasta and cook until the pasta is tender, about 5 minutes. Stir in the remaining basil mixture. Remove the bay leaves, ladle the soup into individual bowls, sprinkle on the cheese, and serve.

Chicken and Pea Soup with Parmesan Dumplings

I use a napkin to enclose the soft dumpling dough here, but some cooks will find a triple layer of rinsed cheesecloth to be just as convenient. Make the soup well ahead of serving, since the dumpling dough needs time to cool to room temperature and then chill before being sliced.

Makes 4 to 6 servings

2 large eggs
About ½ cup all-purpose flour
6 tablespoons grated Parmesan
   cheese, plus additional for
   serving

¼ teaspoon grated nutmeg
¼ teaspoon salt
6 tablespoons butter, softened
8 cups chicken broth
1½ cups fresh or frozen peas

1) In a medium bowl, beat the eggs. Add the flour, 6 tablespoons cheese, nutmeg, and salt and beat well. Beat in the butter to make a soft dough that barely holds its shape when formed into a ball. If the dough seems too soft, beat in more flour. Rinse a large (at least 12-inch) square cotton or linen napkin with water and wring dry. Place the dough in the center of the napkin, bring up the ends of the napkin to form the dough into a ball, and tie the napkin closed at the top with kitchen twine.

2) Meanwhile, in a medium soup pot over high heat, bring the broth to a boil. Plunge the napkin into the soup. Reduce the heat to low and cover partially. Simmer until the ball feels firm, 30 to 40 minutes. Remove the soup from the heat. Remove the ball from the soup and cool to room temperature. When cool, refrigerate for 15 minutes to chill slightly. Unwrap and cut into ½-inch-thick slices. Cut the slices into ¼-inch pieces.

3) Return the broth to a simmer over medium heat. Add the dumplings and cook until heated through, about 10 minutes. Add the peas and cook until tender, about 5 minutes. Serve hot, passing a bowl of Parmesan cheese.

Chicken and Tortellini Soup

*T*ortellini in broth (in brodo), *is a trademark of fine Bolognese kitchens. With frozen tortellini from the supermarket, you can make it in minutes. The traditional version is usually served as a first course. But I add* ragaglie di pollo, *a mixture of chicken giblets and livers, to make my version more interesting and filling. The soup is at its best with a good, homemade chicken broth.*

Makes 6 to 8 servings

1½ tablespoons extra-virgin olive oil
1 medium onion, chopped
8 ounces chicken giblets (hearts and gizzards but not the livers), trimmed and coarsely chopped

8 cups chicken broth
4 ounces chicken livers, trimmed and coarsely chopped
¼ cup dry marsala wine
2 (9-ounce) packages frozen cheese tortellini
Grated Parmesan cheese

1) In a medium soup pot, heat the olive oil over medium heat. Add the onion and cook, stirring often, until softened and translucent, 3 to 5 minutes. Add the giblets and cook, stirring occasionally, until they are lightly browned, 5 to 8 minutes. Add 1 cup of the broth, cover, and reduce the heat to medium-low. Cook until the giblets are tender, about 30 minutes. If more than ¼ cup of the broth remains in the pot, increase the heat to high and boil, uncovered, until reduced to ¼ cup.

2) Stir in the livers. Increase the heat to medium-high. Cook, stirring occasionally, until the livers are lightly browned, about 5 minutes. Add the marsala and cook until the liquid is reduced by half, about 3 minutes.

3) Add the remaining 7 cups broth and bring to a boil over high heat. Stir in the tortellini and cover the pot. Return to a boil and cook until the tortellini are tender, 5 to 8 minutes. Ladle the soup into bowls. Pass grated Parmesan cheese.

Chicken-Vegetable Soup with Tiny Pasta

*T*his lovely minestra is best
made with tender zucchini and young Swiss chard from the
summer garden. It fills the kitchen with one of the most comforting
aromas I can think of. It is light as the air of a spring afternoon,
yet pleasantly filling. **Makes 6 to 8 servings**

2 pounds chicken legs and
  thighs, skinned
3 medium carrots, 1 quartered,
  2 chopped
1 medium onion
2 whole cloves
1 medium celery rib, quartered
2 bay leaves
1 teaspoon salt
10 whole peppercorns, crushed

1 bunch of Swiss chard (about
  2 pounds), stems discarded,
  leaves cut crosswise into
  3-inch strips
½ cup pastina (tiny pasta)
2 medium zucchini, cut into
  ½-inch cubes
Grated Parmesan cheese

1) Place the chicken, quartered carrot, onion studded with the cloves,
celery, bay leaves, salt, and peppercorns in a large soup pot. Add 9 cups
of water. Bring to a boil over high heat, skimming off any foam that rises to
the surface. Reduce the heat to low and simmer until the chicken is
tender, about 1¼ hours.

2) Using a skimmer or a large wire sieve, remove the chicken and
vegetables from the pot. Transfer the vegetables to a blender and puree
in batches. Stir the vegetable puree back into the pot. Remove the chicken
from the bones and tear into shreds.

3) Increase the heat to medium. Add the chopped carrots and cook for
5 minutes. Add the Swiss chard and cook for 5 minutes. Stir in the pastina
and cook 5 minutes. Add the zucchini and cook until the pasta and zucchini
are tender, about 3 minutes. Stir in the chicken. Remove the bay leaves
and ladle the soup into bowls. Pass grated Parmesan cheese on the side.

Farmhouse Winter Soup

*A*ll you need to enjoy this soup is a robust appetite. It is filled with gifts from nature's winter bounty—cabbage, beets, and carrots—as well as chunks of beef, salami, and sausages.   ***Makes 10 servings***

1 cup dried cranberry beans
1 pound beef shin, cut 1 inch thick
8 ounces Genoa salami, peeled and cut into 1-inch chunks
8 ounces sweet Italian sausages, pricked with a fork
1 small head of green cabbage (about 2 pounds), cored and cut into 8 wedges
4 medium celery ribs, chopped

2 medium carrots, chopped
1 large beet, peeled and cut into 1-inch cubes
2 cups chicken broth
½ teaspoon salt
¼ teaspoon freshly ground pepper
1 cup fresh or frozen peas
10 large slices of crusty Italian bread, cut in half and toasted
Grated Parmesan cheese

1) In a large soup pot, cover the beans with at least 2 inches of water. Soak 8 to 24 hours; drain.

2) Return the beans to the soup pot. Add the beef shin, salami, sausages, cabbage, celery, carrots, beet, chicken broth, and 6 cups water. Cover and bring to a boil over high heat, skimming off any foam that rises to the surface. Reduce the heat to low and simmer for 1 hour. Add the salt and pepper and simmer until the beef is tender, about 45 minutes longer.

3) Remove the beef shin and sausages from the soup. Discard the beef bone and cut the meat into 1-inch pieces. Cut the sausages into 1-inch chunks. Return the beef and sausages to the soup. Add the peas and cook until they are tender, about 5 minutes.

4) To serve, place 1 toast in each soup bowl. Ladle the soup into the bowls and top with another toast. Serve immediately. Pass a bowl of Parmesan cheese on the side.

Anna Rosa's Split Pea Soup

Anna Amendolara Nurse, known as Anna Rosa to her friends and family, is one of New York's favorite cooking teachers. She is justifiably famous for her baked ham, as well as for the split pea soup she makes from the ham bones. (I love it when Anna Rosa prepares ham, because she often gives me the bone as a gift!) **Makes 10 servings**

1 pound split peas, rinsed and
  picked over
1 large meaty leftover ham bone
  or 1 (1-pound) ham steak
  with bone
1 large onion, chopped
3 medium carrots, chopped
3 medium celery ribs with
  leaves, chopped

2 garlic cloves, minced
⅓ cup extra-virgin olive oil
1 teaspoon dried thyme
1 bay leaf
½ teaspoon freshly ground
  pepper
1 pound escarole or spinach, well
  rinsed and coarsely chopped
Salt

1) In a large soup pot, combine all of the ingredients except the escarole and salt with 3 quarts water. Bring to a boil over high heat. Reduce the heat to low and simmer, partially covered, stirring occasionally, until the peas are very tender, 2 to 2½ hours.

2) Meanwhile, remove the ham bone from the soup and pull off any meat from the bones. Coarsely chop the meat.

3) Stir the meat back into the soup. Add the escarole or spinach and simmer 8 minutes. Season the soup with salt to taste. Remove and discard the bay leaf. Serve hot.

Tuscan Minestrone

Makes 8 to 12 servings

2 cups dried cannellini or kidney beans

3 tablespoons extra-virgin olive oil

4 ounces thickly sliced prosciutto or ham, chopped

1 medium onion, chopped

1 medium carrot, chopped

1 celery rib, chopped

1 medium leek (white and tender green), well rinsed and chopped

3 garlic cloves—1 minced, 2 crushed through a press

1 tablespoon chopped fresh rosemary or 1½ teaspoons dried

¼ teaspoon crushed hot red pepper

6 cups shredded green or red cabbage

¼ teaspoon salt

¼ teaspoon freshly ground pepper

8 to 12 slices of crusty Italian bread, toasted

½ to ¾ cup grated Parmesan cheese

1) In a large soup pot, cover the beans with at least 2 inches of water. Soak 8 to 24 hours. Drain and rinse well.

2) In the soup pot, heat the olive oil over medium heat. Add the prosciutto, onion, carrot, celery, leek, minced garlic, 2 teaspoons fresh rosemary (or 1 teaspoon dried), and hot pepper. Cook, stirring often, until the vegetables are softened, 5 to 8 minutes. Add the beans. Add 8 cups of water and bring to a boil over high heat. Reduce the heat to low and simmer until the beans are tender, about 1 hour.

3) Add the cabbage, salt, and pepper. Cook until the cabbage is tender, about 20 minutes. Using a slotted spoon, transfer about ½ cup of the vegetables and beans plus a little of the broth to a blender and puree. Return the puree to the pot and stir it in to thicken the soup.

4) In a small bowl, combine the crushed garlic and 1 teaspoon fresh rosemary (or ½ teaspoon dried). Stir into the soup. To serve, place 1 toast in each soup bowl. Ladle in the soup, sprinkle the cheese on top, and serve.

White Beans and Greens Soup

I asked Maria Bucci, a chef at Tuscany's Villa Banfi Winery, about this hearty soup, and she replied, "Cooking is not an exact science, surely not like mathematics . . . a recipe is actually an interpretation." Here's my "interpretation" of her recipe.

Makes 16 servings

1 pound dried cannellini beans
¼ cup extra-virgin olive oil, plus additional for serving
4 medium onions, thinly sliced
6 medium carrots, chopped
6 medium celery ribs, chopped
2 pounds Swiss chard, stems discarded, leaves cut crosswise into 3-inch-wide strips
1 (10-ounce) package spinach, stems removed, rinsed, cut into 2-inch-wide strips

6 ripe plum tomatoes, peeled, seeded, and chopped, or 1 (28-ounce) can peeled tomatoes, drained and chopped
½ teaspoon salt
⅛ teaspoon crushed hot red pepper
16 slices of crusty Italian bread, toasted
Chopped scallions, for garnish

1) In a large soup pot, cover the beans with at least 2 inches of water. Soak 8 to 24 hours. Drain and rinse well.

2) In a large soup pot, heat ¼ cup olive oil over medium heat. Add the onions, carrots, and celery. Cook, stirring often, until the vegetables are soft, about 25 minutes. In batches, add the Swiss chard and spinach, stirring the first batch until wilted before adding the next. Stir in the tomatoes and simmer for 10 minutes.

3) Add 3 quarts water and the beans. Bring to a boil over high heat. Reduce the heat to low and simmer, covered, for 1½ hours. Add the salt and hot pepper. Cook until the beans are soft, about 1 hour longer.

4) To serve, place 1 toast in each soup bowl. Ladle the soup into the bowls and sprinkle with the scallions. Pass a cruet of extra-virgin olive oil on the side, for each guest to drizzle as they wish.

Tomato Soup with Angel Hair Pasta and Mozzarella Cheese

*T**his is a fragrant soup redolent of fresh basil. Make it in the summertime, when the tomatoes are ripe and juicy.*

Makes 6 to 8 servings

2 tablespoons extra-virgin olive oil
1 small onion, finely chopped
2 garlic cloves, crushed through a press
4 pounds ripe plum tomatoes, peeled, seeded, and pureed in a blender or food processor, or use 4 cups canned crushed tomatoes
½ teaspoon salt
¼ teaspoon freshly ground pepper
⅓ cup packed chopped basil leaves
1 teaspoon chopped parsley
1 small zucchini, cut into ½-inch dice
1 cup chicken broth
8 ounces dried angel hair pasta
12 ounces mozzarella cheese, cut into ½-inch cubes

1) In a medium soup pot, heat the olive oil over medium heat. Add the onion and cook, stirring often, until softened and translucent, about 5 minutes. Add half the garlic and cook for 1 minute. Add the tomatoes, 1 cup water, salt, and pepper. Bring to a boil; reduce the heat to low.

2) In a small bowl, mix the basil, parsley, and remaining garlic. Stir 1 tablespoon of this mixture into the soup. Simmer for 10 minutes.

3) Add the zucchini. Bring the soup to a boil, reduce the heat to medium-low, and simmer until the zucchini is barely softened, about 3 minutes.

4) Add 2½ cups water and the broth. Bring to a boil over high heat. Add the pasta, stirring to keep the pasta from sticking together. Cover and cook until the pasta is tender, 3 to 5 minutes. Stir in the remaining basil mixture.

5) Ladle the soup into warm bowls and sprinkle the mozzarella on top. Serve immediately.

Zucchini in Brodo with Poached Eggs

Here's a simple, versatile soup that I like to make when I want a light meal in a hurry. You can use other vegetables instead of zucchini—sliced mushrooms, broccoli or cauliflower florets, or green beans are all good.

Makes 6 servings

2 tablespoons extra-virgin olive oil
1 large onion, chopped
2 medium zucchini, cut into ½-inch dice
2 cups chicken or beef broth

Salt and freshly ground pepper
6 eggs
1 tablespoon grated Parmesan cheese
6 slices of crusty Italian bread, toasted

1) In a large skillet, heat the olive oil over medium-low heat. Add the onion and cook until softened and translucent, 3 to 5 minutes. Add the zucchini and cook, stirring, until just softened, about 3 minutes. Add the broth and bring to a simmer. Season with salt and pepper to taste.

2) Working directly over the skillet, break an egg into the simmering broth. Repeat with the remaining eggs, placing them in a circular pattern with the last egg in the center. Sprinkle with the cheese and cover. Simmer until the egg whites are set, 5 to 8 minutes.

3) To serve, place 1 toast in each soup bowl. Using a slotted spoon, carefully place 1 egg on each slice of toast. Ladle the zucchini and broth into the bowls and serve.

Wild Mushroom and Chestnut Soup

This luxurious soup needs at least three types of mushrooms to achieve its intriguing taste. My favorite combination includes shiitakes, chanterelles, and oyster mushrooms, but the more familiar portobello, cremini, and white button varieties work, too. Dried porcini mushrooms should be a staple in every good cook's pantry. Used sparingly, they add an exquisite flavor to any mushroom dish. To finish the soup in splendor, invest in duck liver pâté, found at specialty grocers', where you sometimes find dried porcini mushrooms for sale in bulk.

Makes 8 servings

1 pound chestnuts

½ ounce dried porcini mushrooms (about ½ cup)

2 ounces pancetta or bacon, chopped

1 tablespoon extra-virgin olive oil

I small onion, sliced

1 small leek (white and tender green), well rinsed and chopped

1 garlic clove, minced

12 ounces mixed fresh wild mushrooms, such as shiitakes (stems discarded), chanterelles, and oyster mushrooms, sliced

9 cups chicken broth

¼ teaspoon salt

¼ teaspoon freshly ground pepper

½ cup heavy cream

4 ounces pâté de foie gras or other liver pâté, cut into ½-inch cubes

Chopped fresh chives or scallions, for garnish

1) Using a small sharp knife, cut a deep "X" in the rounded side of each chestnut, just cutting through the thick outer shell. In a large saucepan of boiling water, cook the chestnuts until the outer skin is split, about 5 minutes. Drain well. While the chestnuts are still warm, peel off the shells. Using the knife, pare off any remaining brown skin. Set the peeled chestnuts aside.

2) Meanwhile, in a small heatproof bowl, cover the dried porcini with 1 cup lukewarm water and let stand until softened, about 15 minutes. Lift out the mushrooms and chop coarsely. Strain the soaking liquid through a sieve lined with a paper towel; set the liquid aside.

3) In a large soup pot, heat the pancetta and olive oil over medium heat until sizzling, about 2 minutes. Add the onion, leek, and garlic and cook, stirring occasionally, until soft, about 5 minutes. Add the fresh mushrooms and cook, stirring often, 5 minutes longer. Add the peeled chestnuts and the chopped porcini with their soaking liquid. Cook, stirring, until half of the liquid evaporates, about 3 minutes.

4) Add the broth, salt, and pepper. Bring to a boil, reduce the heat to low, cover, and simmer, stirring occasionally, until the chestnuts are soft, 35 to 45 minutes. As you stir, use the back of the spoon to crush some of the chestnuts in the pot to thicken the soup slightly. (If desired, at this point puree all of the soup until completely smooth in a food processor or blender. Return to the pot.) Add the cream and cook just until heated through.

5) Place equal amounts of the pâté in individual soup bowls. Ladle in the soup and garnish with the chives. Serve immediately.

Fisherman's Soup with Ham and Vegetables

To be truly authentic, serve this soup with garlicky bruschetta toasts (page 24).

Makes 6 to 8 servings

2 pounds mussels, well scrubbed and debearded
12 littleneck clams, well scrubbed
½ cup dry white wine
2 ounces bacon, coarsely chopped (about ½ cup)
2 ounces prosciutto or smoked ham, coarsely chopped
¼ cup extra-virgin olive oil
1 large red onion, chopped
6 medium scallions, chopped
1 medium leek (white and tender green), cut into thin strips about 2 inches long and well rinsed
3 garlic cloves, minced
2 tablespoons chopped parsley
2 large red potatoes, peeled and cut into 1-inch cubes

½ teaspoon dried thyme
¼ teaspoon freshly ground pepper
4 cups fish stock or 2 cups bottled clam juice and 2 cups water
1 (28-ounce) can crushed tomatoes
½ pound monkfish fillet, cut into 1-inch cubes
½ pound cod fillet, cut into 1-inch cubes
8 ounces medium shrimp, peeled, deveined, and coarsely chopped
4 ounces shelled crabmeat (optional)

1) In a large soup pot, bring the mussels, clams, ¼ cup water, and ¼ cup of the wine to a simmer over medium-low heat. Cover tightly and cook, shaking the pot occasionally, until the shellfish have all opened, 3 to 5 minutes. Discard any unopened shellfish. Pour entire contents of pot into a large bowl. When cool enough to handle, working over the bowl to collect all the juices, discard the shells and place the mussels and clams in a separate bowl. Strain the juices through a wire sieve lined with a moistened paper towel and reserve.

2) Rinse and dry the pot. Add the bacon and ham to the pot and place over medium-high heat. Cook until the bacon is crisp, about 5 minutes. Pour out the fat, leaving the bacon and ham in the pot.

3) Add 2 tablespoons of the olive oil to the pot. Add the red onion, scallions, leek, ⅔ of the minced garlic, and 1 tablespoon parsley. Reduce the heat to medium-low. Cook, stirring often, until the vegetables are softened, about 10 minutes. Add the remaining ¼ cup wine and cook until the wine evaporates, about 3 minutes. Add the potatoes, thyme, and pepper. Cook, stirring often, for 5 minutes.

4) Add the fish stock, crushed tomatoes, and reserved shellfish juices. Cover and bring to a boil over high heat. Add the monkfish and cod and reduce the heat to low. Simmer until the fish is firm, about 10 minutes. Add the shrimp and cook until they turn bright pink, about 2 minutes. Stir in the mussels and clams (add the crabmeat now, if using), the remaining 2 tablespoons oil, 1 tablespoon parsley, and minced garlic. Return to a simmer. Serve immediately.

Shrimp and Mushroom Cacciucco

Makes 6 servings

½ ounce dried porcini mushrooms (about ½ cup)
5 tablespoons extra-virgin olive oil
5 garlic cloves—3 chopped and 2 cut in half
1 pound fresh white mushrooms, coarsely chopped
2 teaspoons chopped fresh mint or ½ teaspoon dried
¼ teaspoon salt

¼ teaspoon freshly ground pepper
1 (28-ounce) can peeled plum tomatoes, drained and finely chopped
1 teaspoon tomato paste
1½ pounds medium shrimp, peeled and deveined
6 slices of crusty Italian bread, toasted

1) In a small bowl, cover the dried porcini with 1 cup lukewarm water and let stand until softened, about 15 minutes. Lift out the mushrooms and chop coarsely. Strain the soaking liquid through a sieve lined with a moistened paper towel and reserve the liquid.

2) In a large soup pot, heat 3 tablespoons of the olive oil over medium heat. Add the chopped garlic and cook until it is softened and fragrant, 1 to 2 minutes. Add the fresh mushrooms, porcini, mint, salt, and pepper. Increase the heat to medium-high and cook until the mushrooms have given off their liquid and they are beginning to brown, 6 to 8 minutes. Stir in the tomatoes and tomato paste. Reduce the heat and simmer 5 minutes.

3) Stir in 4 cups of water and the reserved mushroom liquid. Bring to a boil, reduce the heat to medium-low, and simmer, covered, until slightly thickened, about 45 minutes. Stir in the shrimp and cook until they are curled and bright pink, 3 to 5 minutes.

4) Rub the toast with the cut garlic cloves. Brush the toast with the remaining 2 tablespoons olive oil. Place 1 toast in each soup bowl. Ladle in the soup and serve immediately.

Chicken Broth

Nothing compares with good, old-fashioned, homemade chicken broth. Here's my recipe, which is a little different from others you may have seen. I like to add some veal bones to my broth for extra body, and either fennel or dill for extra flavor. By using a whole chicken, I get poached meat to use in other dishes, but you can use 3 pounds assorted chicken parts if you wish. **Makes 2 to 2½ quarts**

1 large frying chicken
  (3¼ pounds), cut into
  8 pieces
1 pound veal bones
2 medium celery ribs, cut in half
1 medium carrot, cut into
  4 pieces
1 medium onion, studded with
  2 whole cloves and with an
  "X" cut into the root end

6 sprigs of fresh fennel tops or
  dill
3 sprigs of parsley with stems
1 bay leaf
1 teaspoon salt
10 whole peppercorns

1) In a large soup pot, combine all the ingredients and add enough cold water to cover by 2 inches. Bring to a boil over high heat, skimming off any foam that rises to the surface, if desired. Reduce the heat to low, cover, and simmer until the chicken shows no sign of pink at the bone, about 1 hour. Remove the chicken, keeping the broth simmering.

2) Remove the meat from the bones discarding the skin. Save the chicken meat for another use. Return the bones to the pot and continue simmering until the broth is well flavored, about 2 hours.

3) Strain the broth through a colander into a large bowl. If not using immediately, let stand until cool. Cover tightly and refrigerate until ready to use. The broth can be prepared up to 2 days ahead or frozen for up to 3 months.

Fish Broth

Fish broth is so easy to make—
it takes much less time than other classic broths, since the
bones are so delicate. Unfortunately, now that much of our fish
arrives at the supermarkets already cut into fillets, the most
difficult part of making fish broth is finding a fish market that sells
fish heads and bones. Use white, nonoily fish like cod, haddock,
or snapper, as the other varieties (salmon, bluefish, and mackerel)
make an overly strong broth. Whenever you peel raw shrimp at
home, freeze the shells and add them to your pot of fish broth to
add extra flavor. **Makes about 1½ quarts broth**

2 pounds fish heads and bones,
 gills removed, well rinsed
1 large onion, cut into 6 wedges
2 medium celery ribs, chopped
1 medium carrot, chopped

3 sprigs of parsley with stems
2 bay leaves
1 teaspoon salt
10 whole peppercorns

1) In a large soup pot, combine all of the ingredients and add enough
cold water to cover by 1 inch. Bring to a boil over high heat, skimming
off any foam that rises to the surface, if desired. Cover, reduce the heat to
low, and simmer for 30 minutes.

2) Strain the broth through a colander into a large bowl. If not using
immediately, let stand until cool. Cover tightly and refrigerate until
ready to use. The broth can be prepared up to 2 days ahead or frozen for
up to 3 months.

Chicken (and Other Poultry) Italian Style

Traditionally in Italy, chicken, turkeys, and ducks were reserved for festive occasions. But as in America, the popularity of poultry has skyrocketed and luckily, modern production techniques have made it possible for Italians, too, to enjoy them every day. A good thing, since there is no other meat as versatile or as appropriate to one-pot cooking.

Chicken goes especially well with potatoes, rice, and almost any vegetable. It takes well to simmering in wine, tomatoes, or broth. It is good subtly seasoned, sweet and sour, or spiced up with a dose of hot pepper. It loves mushrooms, beans, garlic, and even other meats, such as sausage. From the hearty Chicken with White Beans and Sun-Dried Tomatoes to the Classic Chicken Cacciatora with Olives and Mushrooms, from Turkey Rolls Woodsman Style, stuffed with spinach, cheese, and plenty of mushrooms, to Braised Duck with Olives and Chick-Peas, I've included a one-pot poultry dish for just about every occasion.

In this chapter, you'll see I've also given recipes for Cornish game hens and for rabbit. If you've never tried the latter, I recommend it enthusiastically. This very light meat is lean and delicate, not unlike chicken. You can find rabbit meat at Italian and other fine butcher shops and in the frozen meat section of some supermarkets.

Chicken with White Beans and Sun-Dried Tomatoes

Sun-dried tomatoes are *relatively new to America, but their plump, chewy texture and intense flavor have been a mainstay with Italian cooks for a long time. They are used to perk up food when fresh tomatoes are out of season.*

Makes 4 to 6 servings

½ cup dry-packed sun-dried
  tomatoes
3 tablespoons extra-virgin olive
  oil
2 (3-pound) chickens, cut into
  serving pieces
½ cup dry white wine

½ cup balsamic vinegar
1 teaspoon dried thyme leaves
1 (19-ounce) can cannellini or
  other white beans, drained
  and rinsed
2 small scallions, chopped

1) In a small bowl, soak the sun-dried tomatoes in ½ cup warm water until softened, 10 to 20 minutes. Drain, pat dry, and coarsely chop.

2) In a large flameproof casserole, heat the olive oil over medium-high heat. In batches, add the chicken and cook, turning, until browned all over, about 7 minutes per batch. Pour off all but 2 tablespoons fat.

3) Return the chicken to the pan. Add the wine and cook until almost completely evaporated, 2 to 3 minutes. Stir in ½ cup water, the chopped sun-dried tomatoes, vinegar, and thyme. Reduce the heat to medium-low. Cover and simmer until the chicken is tender and no longer pink near the bone, 35 to 40 minutes.

4) Arrange the chicken around the edges of the pan and pour the beans into the center. Sprinkle with the scallions. Cook, stirring the beans occasionally, until they are heated through, about 5 minutes.

Chicken Cacciatora with Olives and Mushrooms

Makes 4 servings

¼ cup dried porcini mushrooms
3 tablespoons extra-virgin olive
  oil
3 garlic cloves, smashed
1 (3½-pound) frying chicken, cut
  into serving pieces
3 tablespoons chopped celery
  leaves or celery
1 sprig of parsley plus
  1 tablespoon chopped

½ cup dry white wine
2 tablespoons white or red wine
  vinegar
2 bay leaves
1½ cups Gaeta or Kalamata
  olives, pitted if desired
2 flat anchovy fillets packed in
  oil, drained and minced

1) In a small bowl, cover the dried mushrooms with 1 cup warm water. Let stand until softened, about 15 minutes. Lift the mushrooms out of the soaking liquid, squeeze excess water back into bowl, and chop the mushrooms coarsely. Strain the liquid through a paper towel–lined sieve and reserve.

2) In a large skillet, heat the olive oil over medium-high heat. Add 1 clove of garlic and cook until golden brown, 2 to 3 minutes. Discard the garlic. Add the chicken and cook, turning, until well browned all over, 7 to 10 minutes. Add the remaining garlic, celery leaves, parsley sprig, and bay leaves to the skillet. Cook until the garlic is just golden, about 2 minutes. Add the wine and vinegar and cook until almost completely evaporated, about 5 minutes.

3) Add the olives, chopped mushrooms, and anchovies. Cook, stirring, 1 to 2 minutes. Pour in the reserved soaking liquid; reduce the heat to medium-low and cover partially. Cook gently until the chicken is no longer pink in the center, 35 to 40 minutes. Discard the parsley sprig and bay leaves. Sprinkle with the chopped parsley and serve.

Sautéed Chicken alla Friuli

I learned this recipe from Lidia Bastianich, the simpatica owner (with her husband Felice) of the excellent Manhattan restaurant Felidia, which features food from the Friuli region in the north of Italy. Because it has a tasty sauce full of bits of meat, I suggest serving this with polenta.

Makes 4 servings

1 (3½-pound) frying chicken with its liver reserved, cut into serving pieces
¼ teaspoon salt
¼ teaspoon freshly ground pepper
¼ cup extra-virgin olive oil
1 large onion, chopped

2 ounces pancetta or bacon, minced
½ teaspoon dried rosemary
Pinch of ground cloves
2 bay leaves
1 tablespoon tomato paste
1 cup dry white wine
1½ cups chicken broth

1) Season the chicken with the salt and pepper. In a large, deep skillet or flameproof casserole, heat the olive oil over medium-high heat. Add the chicken and cook, turning, until browned all over, 5 to 7 minutes. Remove the chicken from the pan and set aside.

2) Trim and mince the liver. Add the onion, chicken liver, pancetta, rosemary, cloves, and bay leaves. Reduce the heat to medium. Cook, stirring often, until the onion is soft and golden brown, 5 to 7 minutes. Add the tomato paste and wine to the skillet. Stir with a wooden spoon, scraping up the browned bits on the bottom of the pan. Cook for 5 minutes. Stir in the broth. Return the chicken to the skillet.

3) Cover partially and reduce the heat to medium-low. Simmer, turning occasionally, until the chicken is tender and no longer pink in the center, 35 to 40 minutes. Discard the bay leaves before serving.

Chicken Marsala with Garlic and Peas

*T**en garlic cloves may sound like a lot, but don't be concerned. The long simmering renders it gentle as a breeze off the Mediterranean coast. When you want to thaw frozen peas in a hurry, place the peas in a wire sieve and rinse under warm water for a minute or so.* **Makes 4 servings**

1 (4-pound) frying chicken, cut into serving pieces
½ teaspoon salt
¼ teaspoon freshly ground pepper
3 tablespoons extra-virgin olive oil
10 garlic cloves, peeled and crushed
½ cup dry Marsala wine
½ cup chicken broth
½ teaspoon dried basil
2 cups thawed frozen peas
1 tablespoon chopped parsley

1) Season the chicken pieces with the salt and pepper. In a large skillet, heat the olive oil over medium-high heat. Add the chicken and cook, turning, until browned all over, about 7 minutes. Pour off all the fat.

2) Tuck the garlic cloves under and around the chicken. Cook, shaking the pan often, until the garlic is fragrant, 1 to 2 minutes. Add the Marsala, broth, and basil. Bring to a boil, scraping up the browned bits on the bottom of the skillet with a wooden spoon.

3) Reduce the heat to medium-low. Cover and cook, turning the chicken occasionally, until the pieces are tender with no pink in the center, 35 to 40 minutes. Add the peas during the last 3 minutes to heat them through. Sprinkle with the parsley and serve.

Chicken Stew with Green Beans, Wine, and Prosciutto

*T*oss some ingredients into *a pot on the stove and return to a beautifully seasoned, aromatic stew. This chicken comes out juicy, with a savory, finger-licking sauce. And it is cooked with no oil or butter. Serve with polenta.*

Makes 4 servings

1 (4-pound) chicken, cut into
  serving pieces
1 cup dry red wine
¼ cup dry Marsala wine
2 large red potatoes, peeled and
  cut into 1-inch cubes
2 ounces thickly sliced
  prosciutto, finely diced
2 garlic cloves, finely chopped
½ teaspoon dried oregano

3 fresh sage leaves or ½ teaspoon
  dried rubbed sage
⅛ teaspoon ground cloves
2 bay leaves
7 peppercorns, cracked
¼ to ½ teaspoon crushed hot
  pepper flakes, to taste
Salt (optional)
½ pound green beans, cut into
  1-inch lengths

1) Place all of the ingredients except the salt and green beans in a large flameproof casserole. Cover and cook over medium heat 45 minutes.

2) Taste and add salt if needed (the prosciutto is often salty enough). Add the green beans and continue cooking until the chicken is no longer pink at the center and the beans are tender, 10 to 15 additional minutes. Remove the bay leaves before serving.

Roast Chicken with Prosciutto and Potatoes

Here's a classic with many twists. Prosciutto covers the breast, flavoring and moistening the chicken, while the rosemary-seasoned potatoes roast in the pan. Vegetables are also cooked inside the bird, and these are turned into a delicious sauce.

Makes 6 servings

1 (6- to 7-pound) roasting chicken, rinsed and patted dry
1 teaspoon salt
½ teaspoon freshly ground pepper
½ lemon
1 medium onion, quartered
4 medium carrots—quartered, 3 cut into long sticks
4 medium celery ribs—quartered, 3 cut into long sticks

3 tablespoons extra-virgin olive oil
4 thin slices of prosciutto
3 large Idaho baking potatoes, peeled and cut into 6 wedges each
1 garlic clove, sliced
2 teaspoons chopped fresh rosemary or 1 teaspoon dried
¾ cup dry white wine

1) Preheat the oven to 400 degrees F. Season the chicken inside and out with ½ teaspoon salt and ¼ teaspoon pepper. Squeeze the lemon juice over the chicken and place the lemon shell in the body cavity, along with the quartered onion and cut-up carrot and celery. Massage the chicken with 1 tablespoon of the olive oil. Truss the chicken with kitchen string. Arrange the carrot and celery sticks in the center of the roasting pan and place the chicken on top. Drape overlapping slices of prosciutto over the breast of the chicken.

2) In a large bowl, toss the potatoes with the garlic, rosemary, and remaining 2 tablespoons oil, ½ teaspoon salt, and ¼ teaspoon pepper. Arrange the potatoes around the chicken.

3) Roast for 20 minutes. Reduce the oven temperature to 375 degrees. Continue to roast, turning the potatoes and basting the chicken with ½ cup wine and the pan juices occasionally, until the juices from the chicken run clear yellow when pierced in the thigh, 1¾ to 2 hours longer. Remove the chicken to a carving board and remove the strings. Transfer the vegetables with the juices from the chicken cavity to a blender or food processor and puree until smooth. Cut the carrots and celery in pieces and combine with the potatoes; transfer to a warm serving bowl.

4) Place the roasting pan on top of the stove over low heat. Pour in the remaining ¼ cup wine and 2 tablespoons water and scrape up the browned bits in the pan with a wooden spoon. Stir in the pureed vegetables and cook until hot. Season the sauce with salt and pepper to taste and pour into a sauceboat. Carve the chicken. Pass the vegetables and sauce on the side.

Roast Chicken Casalinga with Peppers and Olives

his homey dish is adapted from a recipe of chef Antonio Stanziani from Villa Santa Maria, a town in Abruzzo that is famous for its chefs' cooking school, which originated in the Middle Ages. ***Makes 4 to 6 servings***

1 (5-pound) roasting chicken, rinsed and patted dry
½ teaspoon salt
¼ teaspoon freshly ground pepper
2 sprigs of fresh rosemary or 1 teaspoon dried
2 garlic cloves, unpeeled, crushed lightly

2 tablespoons extra-virgin olive oil
1 cup dry white wine
4 large bell peppers, preferably red, green, and yellow, cut into 1-inch squares
1 cup black Mediterranean olives, pitted

1) Preheat the oven to 400 degrees F. Rinse and dry the chicken. Sprinkle the chicken inside and out with the salt and pepper. Place 1 rosemary sprig and the garlic in the large cavity. Truss the chicken with kitchen string and massage with the olive oil. Set on a rack in a roasting pan and pour ½ cup water into the pan.

2) Roast for 30 minutes. Reduce the oven temperature to 350 degrees. Pour the wine over the chicken and roast, basting occasionally with the pan juices, for another 30 minutes.

3) Add the peppers, olives, and remaining rosemary sprig to the pan. Continue to roast, stirring the peppers once or twice, until the juices from the chicken run clear yellow when pierced in the thigh, 30 to 45 minutes longer. Let the chicken stand for 5 to 10 minutes before carving.

Sausage-Stuffed Chicken Cutlets with Spinach

*C*hicken breasts can be stuffed
*with many different ingredients, but sausage stuffings are hard
to surpass. Sometimes I will roll a spinach leaf or two up in the
breast along with the filling, as it adds a little color and looks
nice. If you have any* rollatine *left over, serve them cold, cut into
thin rounds.* **Makes 4 to 6 servings**

¾ pound Italian-style chicken or
   turkey sausages, casings
   removed
1 egg, lightly beaten
8 skinless, boneless chicken
   cutlets
8 strips of bacon

1 tablespoon extra-virgin olive
   oil
¼ cup dry Marsala wine
1 tablespoon butter
2 pounds spinach, well rinsed,
   tough stems removed
Salt and freshly ground pepper

1) In a small bowl, mix the sausage and egg. Divide the sausage mixture
evenly among the chicken cutlets. Roll up each chicken cutlet, wrap
each with 1 bacon strip, and secure with a toothpick.

2) In a large skillet, heat the olive oil over medium-high heat. In batches,
cook the chicken, turning, until lightly browned on both sides, 5 to
7 minutes. Remove the chicken to a plate. Add the Marsala and bring to a
boil, scraping up any browned bits on the bottom of the pan. Return the
chicken to the skillet.

3) Reduce the heat to medium-low, cover, and cook until the chicken is
no longer pink in the center, 10 to 15 minutes. Remove the breasts to a
platter and cover with foil. Boil the liquid in the skillet until it is evaporated
to about 1 tablespoon.

4) Add the butter and increase the heat to high. Add the spinach with
any water clinging to its leaves. Cook, stirring, until just tender but still
bright green, 2 to 3 minutes. Season with salt and pepper to taste. Arrange the
spinach around the chicken and serve.

Ragout of Chicken Legs
and Sausages

A small amount of dried *porcini boosts the flavor of ordinary fresh mushrooms tremendously, so I use them a lot. To keep the fat low, I like to take the skin off the chicken. These days, many supermarkets sell drumsticks already skinned.*

Makes 6 servings

¼ cup dried porcini mushrooms
2 tablespoons extra-virgin olive
   oil
½ pound sweet Italian sausage,
   casings removed
½ cup flour
½ teaspoon dried rosemary,
   crumbled
½ teaspoon salt

¼ teaspoon freshly ground
   pepper
12 chicken drumsticks, skin
   removed
½ cup dry red wine
1 teaspoon tomato paste
1 pound fresh mushrooms, sliced
1 tablespoon chopped parsley

1) In a small bowl, cover the dried mushrooms with ½ cup lukewarm water. Let stand until softened, about 15 minutes. Lift the mushrooms out of the soaking liquid and chop coarsely. Strain the liquid through a paper towel–lined sieve and reserve.

2) In a shallow flameproof casserole, heat the olive oil over medium-high heat. Add the sausage and cook, stirring occasionally, until lightly browned. Use a slotted spoon to remove to a plate.

3) In a large plastic storage bag, combine the flour, rosemary, salt, and pepper. In batches, add the chicken and shake to coat with the flour. Add to the drippings in the casserole and cook, turning, until browned all over, about 8 minutes. Remove to the plate with the sausage.

4) Add the wine and tomato paste to the casserole; stir up the browned bits from the bottom of the pan. Boil until almost completely evaporated. Add the fresh mushrooms and soaked mushrooms to the casserole. Cook, stirring often, until the mushrooms release their liquid and it evaporates, 7 to 10 minutes. Return the chicken and sausage to the pan. Stir in half of the reserved mushroom soaking liquid.

5) Reduce the heat to medium-low and cover. Cook gently, adding the remaining mushroom soaking liquid after 15 minutes, until the chicken is no longer pink in the center, 35 to 40 minutes. Serve garnished with parsley.

Chicken in Prison

T*his is my adaptation of a classic Sicilian preparation in which the chicken is enclosed in a loaf of bread. Legend has it that this unusual dish was created by an Arab emir during the Moorish rule of Sicily.*

Makes 8 servings

1 (3½-pound) chicken, cut into
   serving pieces
¼ teaspoon salt
¼ teaspoon freshly ground
   pepper
3 tablespoons extra-virgin olive
   oil
1 medium onion, chopped
2 cups chicken broth
2 tablespoons slivered almonds

2 tablespoons pine nuts
1 large round loaf of crusty
   Italian bread (about
   1½ pounds)
2 eggs
2 tablespoons fresh lemon juice
2 tablespoons capers, coarsely
   chopped
1 tablespoon chopped parsley

1) Season the chicken with salt and pepper. In a large skillet, heat the olive oil over medium-high heat. Add the chicken and cook, turning, until browned all over, about 7 minutes. Add the onion and cook, stirring often, until softened and translucent, 3 to 5 minutes. Add 1 cup of the broth and bring to a boil. Reduce the heat to low. Cover and simmer, gradually adding another ½ cup broth, until the chicken is no longer pink at the bone, about 35 minutes. Remove the chicken, reserving the cooking liquid. Discard the skin and bones and coarsely chop the chicken meat.

2) Preheat the oven to 350 degrees F. Place the almonds and pine nuts on a baking sheet and bake, stirring often, until fragrant and lightly toasted, 6 to 8 minutes. Let cool completely, then chop coarsely and set aside. Leave the oven on.

3) Cut off the top of the bread. Scoop out the crumbs and place in a large bowl. Add the reserved cooking liquid and remaining ½ cup broth to the bowl. Stir and chop with the side of a large spoon until the mixture is the consistency of thick cream. Add a little additional broth or water if needed. Add the chopped, toasted nuts, eggs, lemon juice, capers, and parsley. Mix well. Stir in the chopped chicken. Fill the bread with this mixture and cover with the bread top. Place on a baking sheet, with a small bowl of water next to the bread (the water will add moisture to the oven and keep the bread crust from becoming too hard).

4) Bake until the loaf is heated through and the filling is firm, about 30 minutes. If the crust is darkening, wrap the loaf in foil. Let cool for 15 minutes before cutting into wedges with a serrated knife. Serve warm or at room temperature.

NOTE: If you have too much stuffing, reserve it and stir it into a soup.

Cool Chicken Breasts with Green Herb Sauce

Makes 6 servings

3 medium leeks (white and
tender green), halved
lengthwise and well rinsed
4 large romaine lettuce leaves
3 medium celery ribs, with leaves
2 lemons—sliced, 1 squeezed to
yield juice
4 sprigs of parsley with stems
2 bay leaves
6 chicken breast halves on the
bone, skinned
½ teaspoon salt

¼ teaspoon freshly ground
pepper
1 cup loosely packed fresh basil
½ cup loosely packed parsley
3 garlic cloves, crushed
1 tablespoon balsamic vinegar
2 or 3 cornichons or small sour
pickles
3 tablespoons extra-virgin olive
oil
2 tablespoons capers, drained
12 cherry tomatoes, halved

1) Place the leeks, lettuce leaves, and celery ribs in a large skillet. Scatter the sliced lemon, parsley sprigs, and bay leaves over the vegetables. Top with the chicken breasts, sprinkle with half the lemon juice, and season with some of the salt and pepper. Add 1 cup water and bring to a simmer over high heat. Reduce the heat to low and cover. Simmer until the chicken is no longer pink in the center, 30 to 35 minutes. Remove the chicken and let cool completely. Discard the lemon slices, bay leaves, and parsley sprigs.

2) Transfer the cooled vegetables with juices from the pan to a blender or food processor. Add the remaining lemon juice, the basil, parsley, garlic, vinegar, and pickles. With the machine on, gradually add the olive oil until the mixture forms a smooth sauce. Season with additional salt and pepper if necessary.

3) Pour half of the sauce onto to a large serving platter. Arrange the chicken on top and spoon the remaining sauce over the chicken. Garnish with the capers and cherry tomatoes. Serve at cool room temperature.

Chicken Livers with Eggs and Sweet Peppers

*C*hicken livers are an inexpensive way to make a quick meal, and if you get them during the right season, sweet peppers can be a bargain, too. The peppers and livers are combined with just enough eggs to set, but not enough to call this a bona fide frittata. **Makes 6 servings**

2 tablespoons extra-virgin olive oil
1 large onion, chopped
½ cup dry white wine
6 bell peppers, preferably red, green, and yellow, cut into thin strips
½ teaspoon marjoram
1½ pounds chicken livers, trimmed and quartered

½ teaspoon salt
¼ teaspoon freshly ground pepper
2 eggs
2 tablespoons dried bread crumbs
2 tablespoons chopped parsley
1 tablespoon capers, drained

1) In a large skillet or flameproof casserole, heat the olive oil over medium-low heat. Add the onion and 2 tablespoons of the wine. Cook, stirring often, until the onion is softened, about 5 to 8 minutes. Add the peppers and marjoram and cook, stirring often, until the peppers are just tender, 8 to 10 minutes.

2) Add the chicken livers and season with half the salt and pepper. Cook, stirring occasionally, until the livers lose their raw look, about 5 minutes. Add the remaining 6 tablespoons wine and increase the heat to medium-high. Cook until the wine is almost completely evaporated, about 3 minutes.

3) In a medium bowl, beat the eggs and mix in the bread crumbs, 1 tablespoon parsley, capers, and remaining salt and pepper. Pour into the skillet and reduce the heat to medium-low. Cook, stirring gently, until the eggs are just set, 3 to 5 minutes. Sprinkle on the remaining parsley and serve.

Oven-Braised Cornish Hens

*I*f the hens come with giblets *(sometimes the producers leave them out), add them to the casserole for extra flavor and puree them right into the sauce. Brown the giblets along with the hens, but add the livers to the casserole only during the last 8 minutes of braising, or they will become bitter and overcooked.* ***Makes 4 servings***

2 Cornish game hens (about
   1½ pounds each), rinsed and
   patted dry
¼ teaspoon salt
¼ teaspoon freshly ground
   pepper
3 tablespoons extra-virgin olive
   oil
¾ cup dry white wine

2 medium onions, quartered
2 medium carrots, cut into
   1-inch pieces
2 medium celery ribs, cut into
   1-inch pieces
¾ cup chicken broth
2 teaspoons finely chopped
   parsley
2 garlic cloves, finely chopped

1) Preheat the oven to 375 degrees F. Season the hens with the salt and pepper. In an oval, flameproof casserole, heat the olive oil over medium-high heat. Add the hens to the casserole and cook, turning, until browned all over, 8 to 10 minutes. Add half of the wine and cook until the wine has almost completely evaporated, 3 to 5 minutes. Add the onion, carrots, celery, and ½ cup broth. Bring to a boil.

2) Cover and place in the oven. Bake, basting occasionally with the remaining ¼ cup broth, wine, and the pan juices, until the juices from the hens run clear yellow when pierced in the thigh, about 1¼ hours. Remove the hens to a carving board and cover with foil to keep warm.

3) Transfer the cooking liquid and half of the vegetables in the casserole to a blender or food processor. Add the parsley and garlic and puree into a smooth sauce. Pour into a sauceboat. Carve the hens in half and arrange on a serving platter. Arrange the remaining vegetables around the hens and serve while hot. Pass the sauce on the side.

Turkey and Zucchini Stew

Turkey's dark meat has a delicate but pronounced flavor that stands up to the seasonings and to the mélange of zucchini, tomatoes, and prosciutto in this savory dish.

Makes 4 to 6 servings

2 tablespoons extra-virgin olive oil
1 large red onion, thinly sliced
4 turkey drumsticks (about 2 pounds), sawed by the butcher into 1-inch-thick pieces
½ cup dry red wine
3 medium zucchini, sliced into ½-inch-thick rounds

2 ounces sliced prosciutto, cut into thin shreds
4 ripe plum tomatoes, cut into ½-inch dice
2 tablespoons chopped fresh basil
1 tablespoon minced fresh parsley
2 garlic cloves, minced
Salt and freshly ground pepper

1) In a large flameproof casserole, heat the olive oil over medium-high heat. Add the onion and cook, stirring occasionally, until softened and translucent, 3 to 5 minutes. Add the turkey and cook, turning, until the meat starts to brown, 3 to 5 minutes longer. Add the wine and cook until almost completely evaporated, about 5 minutes. Add 1 cup water and bring to a boil. Reduce the heat to medium-low. Cook, adding more water if needed, until the turkey is almost tender, about 1¼ hours.

2) Add the zucchini, prosciutto, and tomatoes and cook until the turkey and zucchini are tender, about 10 minutes. Stir in the basil, parsley, and garlic. Season the sauce with salt and pepper to taste and serve.

Turkey Rolls Woodsman Style

Involtini, *or stuffed rolls of all kinds of meats, are popular in Italy. "Woodsman-style" dishes are made with an abundance of mushrooms, preferably the wild variety. Dried porcini add their earthy flavor to cultivated mushrooms and to these cheese-stuffed turkey rolls.*

Makes 4 to 6 servings

½ cup dried porcini mushrooms (about 1 ounce)
¼ cup extra-virgin olive oil
1 medium onion, chopped
1 pound fresh mushrooms, sliced
2 cups shredded mozzarella cheese
1 (10-ounce) package frozen chopped spinach, thawed and squeezed of excess moisture

1 egg, beaten
2 tablespoons dried bread crumbs
¼ teaspoon salt
¼ teaspoon freshly ground pepper
2 pounds turkey breast cutlets, pounded thin (12 pieces)
½ cup dry white wine
1 tablespoon chopped fresh parsley

1) In a small bowl, cover the dried mushrooms with 1 cup lukewarm water. Let stand until softened, about 15 minutes. Lift the mushrooms out of the soaking liquid and chop coarsely. Strain the liquid through a paper towel–lined sieve and reserve.

2) In a large skillet, heat 2 tablespoons of the olive oil over medium heat. Add the onion and cook until just softened, 2 to 3 minutes. Add the sliced fresh mushrooms and the porcini. Cook until the fresh mushrooms give off their liquid, the liquid evaporates, and the mushrooms begin to brown, 8 to 10 minutes. Remove to a bowl and set aside. Carefully wipe the skillet clean with paper towels.

3) In a medium bowl, combine the mozzarella, spinach, egg, bread crumbs, salt, and pepper. Mix to blend well. Spread the mixture evenly over the turkey cutlets, leaving a ½-inch border around the edges. Roll up each cutlet and secure each with a toothpick.

4) In the cleaned skillet, heat the remaining 2 tablespoons oil over medium heat. Add the turkey rolls and cook, turning, until browned all over, 5 to 7 minutes. Add ¼ cup of the wine and boil until evaporated, about 2 minutes. Add the mushroom soaking liquid and bring to a boil. Reduce the heat to medium-low, cover, and cook until the turkey is tender and shows no sign of pink in the center, 25 to 30 minutes. Remove to a plate and cover with foil to keep warm.

5) Pour the remaining ¼ cup wine into the skillet. Increase the heat to high and boil until the liquid evaporates to about ⅓ cup. Return the turkey rolls and mushrooms to the skillet and toss until heated through, about 2 minutes. Sprinkle with the parsley and serve.

Duck Stew Perugia-Style

This is one of Perugia's best-known dishes—duck soaked in a hardy white wine and brandy marinade, then turned into an aromatic stew. The longer the duck marinates, the better, so plan ahead, allow at least 3 hours, or prepare through step 2 a day ahead.   ***Makes 4 servings***

1 duck (about 5 pounds), trimmed of excess fat and skin, cut into serving pieces
1 large onion, chopped
1 cup dry white wine
2 tablespoons Cognac or brandy
¼ teaspoon ground cloves
¼ teaspoon freshly ground pepper

¼ teaspoon salt
¾ pound fresh mushrooms, sliced
2 tablespoons finely chopped prosciutto
1 garlic clove, minced
2 bay leaves
1 tablespoon chopped parsley

1) In a large flameproof casserole, cook the duck pieces over medium heat, turning, until the duck renders most of its fat and the skin is golden brown, 10 to 15 minutes. Drain the duck on paper towels. Pour the fat out of the pan.

2) Return the duck to the casserole. Add the onion, wine, Cognac, cloves, and pepper. Cover and refrigerate, turning the duck occasionally, for at least 3 hours or overnight.

3) Bring the casserole to a boil over high heat. Cover, reduce the heat to low, and simmer 1 to 1½ hours, or until the duck is tender.

4) Add the mushrooms, prosciutto, garlic, and bay leaves. Increase the heat to medium and cook 10 to 15 minutes, until the mushrooms are tender. Discard the bay leaves, sprinkle with the parsley, and serve.

Braised Duck with Olives and Chick-Peas

Makes 4 servings

1 duck (about 5 pounds),
   trimmed of excess fat and
   skin, cut into serving pieces
2 tablespoons extra-virgin olive
   oil
1 teaspoon chopped fresh
   rosemary or ½ teaspoon
   dried
1 teaspoon chopped fresh sage
   leaves or ½ teaspoon dried
3 garlic cloves, sliced
¼ teaspoon crushed hot pepper
   flakes, or more to taste

1 cup dry white wine
2 bay leaves
1 (16-ounce) can peeled Italian
   tomatoes, coarsely chopped,
   juices reserved
1 (19-ounce) can chick-peas,
   rinsed and drained
¾ cup Mediterranean green
   olives, pitted if desired
1 tablespoon chopped parsley

1) Bring a large flameproof casserole of water to a boil over high heat. Add the duck and remove from the heat. Let stand for about 10 minutes. Drain the duck, discarding the water. Dry the pot with paper towels.

2) In the same pot, heat the olive oil over medium-high heat. Add the duck and cook, turning occasionally, until browned all over, 10 to 15 minutes. Pour off all but 1 tablespoon fat. Add the rosemary, sage, garlic, and hot pepper. Cook, stirring, until the garlic colors, 1 to 2 minutes. Immediately add the wine and bay leaves and boil until the wine is almost completely evaporated. Stir in the tomatoes with their juices and bring to a boil; reduce the heat to low.

3) Cover and simmer, turning the duck occasionally, until it shows no sign of pink at the bone, about 1 hour. Stir in the chick-peas and olives and cook until heated through, about 3 minutes. Discard the bay leaves, sprinkle with the parsley, and serve.

Old-Fashioned Rabbit with Rice

Rabbit is rabbit, and chicken
is chicken, but I can safely say this is one dish that is excellent
with either. The house will be filled with that unmistakable scent
of tomatoes and basil that sings out "old-fashioned Italian cooking!"

Makes 4 servings

1 rabbit (about 3 pounds), cut
   into serving pieces
Salt and freshly ground pepper
2 tablespoons extra-virgin olive
   oil
¼ pound pancetta or slab bacon,
   rind removed, cut into
   ¼-inch dice
1 cup dry white wine

2 cups chicken broth
1 (16-ounce) can peeled
   tomatoes, coarsely chopped,
   juices reserved
3 tablespoons chopped fresh
   basil
6 ounces Gaeta or Kalamata
   olives, pitted
1 cup converted rice

1) Season the rabbit with ¼ teaspoon each of salt and pepper. In a large
flameproof casserole, cook the olive oil and pancetta over medium heat
until the pancetta is lightly browned, about 5 minutes. Use a slotted spoon to
remove the pancetta to paper towels, leaving the fat in the casserole.

2) Increase the heat to medium-high. Add the rabbit and cook, turning,
until browned all over, about 7 minutes. Remove the rabbit from the
skillet and set aside. Add the wine, scraping up any browned bits from the
bottom of the pan. Boil until the liquid is almost completely evaporated,
about 8 minutes. Stir in the broth, tomatoes with their juices. 1½ tablespoons
of the basil, the olives, and rice. Bring to a boil over high heat. Return the
rabbit to the skillet.

3) Reduce the heat to low, cover, and simmer, stirring once in a
while, until the rabbit and rice are tender, about 1 hour. Season with salt
and pepper to taste. Sprinkle the remaining basil over the top and serve.

Beef and Veal all'Italiana

Italian skillet dishes and stews comprise most of these savory one-pot dishes. Many, such as Steak alla Pizzaiola and Veal Scaloppine with Prosciutto, Peas, and Artichoke Hearts, cook in a flash. Others require longer, slower simmering, but they cook with little attention, and the succulent results are well worth the wait. You'll find recipes like Southern Italian Beef Rollatine with Pasta Shells, Pine Nuts, and Raisins and Country-Style Osso Buco.

In Italy, we always serve our pasta first and then present the meat by itself, sometimes with a green vegetable or a salad following or on the side. A couple of these recipes adhere to such a menu format, but we are also very inventive when it comes to stews and to stretching meat. After all, for years beef and, of course, baby veal, were very scarce. I've pulled out many of these more substantial meat dishes from my repertoire or added a little something extra to a classic to turn it into a one-dish meal, such as the potatoes in the Country-Style Osso Buco.

This chapter contains beef and veal recipes for a variety of occasions. For everyday meals, there are my own family favorites, like Savory Meatballs with Sweet Peppers and Veal, Red Onion, and Potato Casserole. You'll also find regional classics, such as Tuscan Pot Roast with Mustard and Florentine Beef Stew with Potatoes, and even elegant dishes for entertaining, such as Veal Scaloppine with Prosciutto, Peas, and Artichoke Hearts.

Steak alla Pizzaiola

When dishes are served *alla pizzaiola, it's not hard to conclude that the sauce includes tomatoes, garlic, and oregano—some of the most popular ingredients on a pizza. This sauce is a classic of Neapolitan cooking and is supposed to cook quickly, dispelling the notion that all tomato sauces must cook for hours. Serve with steamed broccoli.* **Makes 6 servings**

3 tablespoons extra-virgin olive oil
6 boneless sirloin, club, or rib steaks (about 8 ounces each)
4 garlic cloves, thinly sliced
¼ teaspoon salt
⅛ teaspoon freshly ground pepper
½ cup dry red wine

1 (16-ounce) can peeled tomatoes, coarsely chopped, juices reserved
2 tablespoons chopped parsley
1 teaspoon dried oregano
⅛ teaspoon crushed hot pepper flakes
1 pound mozzarella cheese, cut into 1-inch cubes

1) In a large skillet, heat the olive oil over high heat until very hot but not smoking. Add the steaks and cook until the undersides are browned, 2 to 3 minutes. Add the garlic, turn the steaks over, and cook until the other sides are browned, about 2 minutes. Remove to a platter, leaving the oil in the skillet. Season the steaks with the salt and pepper.

2) Add the wine to the skillet and cook until it just evaporates, about 3 minutes. Add the tomatoes with their juices, 1 tablespoon of the parsley, the oregano, and hot pepper. Bring to a boil and cook over medium heat, stirring occasionally, until thickened, 8 to 10 minutes.

3) Return the steaks and any juices that have collected on the platter to the skillet. Scatter the mozzarella cubes over the steaks and baste with the sauce. Cover and cook over medium heat until the mozzarella begins to melt, about 2 minutes. Sprinkle with the remaining 1 tablespoon parsley and serve immediately.

Filets Mignons in a Skillet

This old recipe dates back to
the eighteenth century, when the Bourbons of France ruled
Abruzzo. Unlike many ornate court dishes of the period, this one
is quite simple and very contemporary in taste. Serve with a
simple salad or sautéed spinach or escarole. **Makes 6 servings**

1 tablespoon extra-virgin olive
  oil
1 tablespoon unsalted butter
6 filets mignons, cut ¾ inch thick
  (about 1¾ pounds)
¼ teaspoon salt
¼ teaspoon freshly ground
  pepper

¼ cup dry white wine
3 tablespoons dry Marsala
4 ounces mozzarella cheese, cut
  into 6 slices
6 flat anchovy fillets packed in
  oil, drained
6 thick slices of crusty Italian
  bread, toasted

1) In a large skillet, heat the olive oil and butter over medium-high heat
until very hot but not smoking. Add the steaks and cook, turning once,
until browned on both sides, about 4 minutes total. Season the meat with the
salt and pepper.

2) Add the wine and Marsala and cook until evaporated by half, 1 to
2 minutes. Turn the fillets and top each with 1 mozzarella slice and
1 anchovy fillet. Cover partially and cook until the mozzarella is melted,
about 2 minutes. Place a slice of toast on each dinner plate. Top each
toast with a filet mignon.

Florentine Beef Stew with Potatoes

The Florentines have a knack for cooking beef, certainly because the best steer in Italy is from Tuscany. This kind of saucy stew is called a stufatino. While it is often served with polenta, I prefer to cook potatoes right in the same pot.

Makes 4 to 6 servings

3 tablespoons extra-virgin olive oil
2 pounds trimmed beef stew meat, such as chuck, cut into 1-inch cubes
½ teaspoon salt
¼ teaspoon freshly ground pepper
1 medium onion, chopped
1 medium carrot, chopped
1 medium celery rib, chopped
¾ cup dry red wine
1 (16-ounce) can peeled tomatoes, coarsely chopped, juices reserved
1 teaspoon tomato paste
2 tablespoons chopped fresh basil
2 tablespoons chopped parsley
3 medium potatoes, peeled and cut into ½-inch cubes

1) In a large Dutch oven, heat the olive oil over medium-high heat. Add the meat in 2 or 3 batches and cook, turning the pieces occasionally, until browned on all sides, 6 to 8 minutes per batch. Return all the beef to the pot. Season with the salt and pepper.

2) Add the onion, chopped carrot, and celery to the pot and reduce the heat to medium. Cook, stirring often, until the vegetables begin to soften, about 5 minutes. Add the wine and bring to a boil, scraping up the browned bits from the bottom of the pan. Cook until the wine evaporates, 4 to 6 minutes. Add the tomatoes with their juices, the tomato paste, 1 tablespoon basil, and 1 tablespoon parsley.

3) Cover and reduce the heat to low. Simmer, stirring occasionally, 1 hour. Add the potatoes and simmer 30 to 45 minutes longer. Sprinkle with the remaining basil and parsley. Serve immediately.

Southern Italian Beef Rollatine with Pasta Shells, Pine Nuts, and Raisins

In Apulia, one of the *southernmost Italian regions, the cooks use a special seasoning of pine nuts, raisins, garlic, and parsley in many recipes. Here these ingredients flavor a filling for beef rollatine simmered in tomato sauce. Serve them over pasta, preferably cavatelli, which can be found in the freezer department of Italian grocery stores and many supermarkets, or dried orecchiette.* ***Makes 6 servings***

2 tablespoons raisins
2 tablespoons chopped parsley
1½ tablespoons pine nuts
2 garlic cloves, slivered
2 ounces Romano cheese in
  1 chunk, cut in as many thin
  strips as there are beef slices
2 ounces sliced pancetta, cut
  into as many thin strips as
  there are beef slices
1 bottom or top round beef roast,
  cut across the grain into
  ¼-inch-thick slices, then
  pounded thin (1¾ pounds)

Freshly ground pepper
3 tablespoons olive oil
1 large onion, thinly sliced
½ cup dry red wine
1 (28-ounce) can tomato puree
1 teaspoon dried sage
Salt
1 pound frozen cavatelli or dried
  small pasta shells
Grated Romano cheese

1) In a small bowl, combine the raisins, 1 tablespoon of the parsley, the pine nuts, and the garlic. Place 1 strip of Romano cheese and 1 strip of pancetta in the center of each beef slice. Sprinkle equal amounts of the raisin mixture onto each slice, leaving a ½-inch border around the edges. Season with a generous grinding of pepper. Fold in both short sides about

½ inch. Starting at a long side, roll up the slices into thick cylinders and tie with kitchen string

2) In a large Dutch oven, heat the olive oil over medium heat. Add the onion and cook, stirring, until softened, about 3 minutes. Add the beef rolls to the pot and cook, turning, until they are lightly browned all over, about 10 minutes.

3) Pour in the wine and cook until it evaporates, about 3 minutes. Stir in the tomato puree, sage, and 1½ cups water. Bring to a simmer and reduce the heat to low. Cover and cook, turning the rolls occasionally in the sauce, until they are tender, 2 to 2½ hours. Remove the rollatine to a deep bowl. Skim any fat off the sauce, season with salt and pepper to taste, and pour over the meat. Cover with foil to keep warm. Clean the pot.

4) In the same pot, bring 4 quarts of water to a rapid boil. Add salt and the pasta and cook until tender but still firm, 8 to 10 minutes. Drain the pasta in a colander and return it to the pot. Add 2 cups of the sauce and toss to coat the pasta lightly (the pasta shouldn't swim in the sauce). Pour the remaining sauce into a sauceboat. Transfer the pasta to a deep serving bowl and top with the rollatine. Sprinkle with the remaining 1 tablespoon parsley and serve, passing the sauce and a bowl of Romano cheese.

Tuscan Pot Roast with Mustard

*T*his zesty Tuscan specialty has a couple of tricks to its preparation. First, use a high-quality grainy mustard, such as French Pommery. Also, cook the roast slowly in a heavy-bottomed casserole with very little liquid— the Italians say in umido, *or with humidity. A flame-tamer may come in handy to maintain low, even heat. If the liquid boils away too fast, just add a few tablespoons broth or water. Like all pot roasts, this tastes even better the next day.*

Makes 6 to 8 servings

1 beef top or bottom round roast, tied (4 pounds)
1 tablespoon grainy mustard, such as Pommery
2 tablespoons all-purpose flour
2 tablespoons butter
1 tablespoon extra-virgin olive oil

¾ cup dry red wine
½ teaspoon salt
⅛ teaspoon freshly ground pepper
1 pound small red potatoes, scrubbed and halved

1) Spread the meat with the mustard, then sprinkle all over with the flour. In a large flameproof casserole, heat the butter and olive oil over medium heat. Add the roast to the pot. Cook, turning occasionally, until the meat is nicely browned, 10 to 15 minutes.

2) Pour in the wine and bring to a boil. Boil until the wine is reduced by half. Add ½ cup water and the salt and pepper. Cover and reduce the heat to low. Cook, turning the roast occasionally, for 2½ hours. Check the pot and add water as needed to keep the meat moist.

3) Add the potatoes and more water if necessary. Cover and continue cooking until the meat is fork-tender and the potatoes are done, 30 to 40 minutes. Let the roast stand for 10 minutes before slicing.

Oxtail Stew alla Vaccinara

Outside the portals of Rome, in the countryside where beef was once raised, many trattorie still serve this ancient dish. The name has its roots in the word vaccaro, or cowboy.

Makes 6 to 8 servings

¼ cup lard or 2 ounces minced
   pancetta or bacon
3 medium carrots—1 quartered,
   2 cut into ½-inch dice
3 medium celery ribs—
   1 quartered, 2 cut into
   ½-inch dice
2 garlic cloves, finely chopped
2 sprigs of parsley
1 tablespoon extra-virgin olive
   oil
½ cup all-purpose flour

¾ teaspoon salt
¼ teaspoon freshly ground
   pepper
5 pounds oxtails, cut into 1-inch-
   thick pieces
½ cup dry red wine
1 tablespoon tomato paste
1 (28-ounce) can peeled
   tomatoes, coarsely chopped,
   juices reserved
2 bay leaves

1) In a food processor, combine the lard or pancetta, the quartered carrot and celery, the garlic, and the parsley. Process until the vegetables are minced. In a large flameproof casserole, heat the olive oil over medium heat. Add the lard and vegetable mixture and cook, stirring often, 5 minutes.

2) In a deep dish, mix the flour, salt, and pepper. Dredge the oxtails in the seasoned flour. Add the oxtails to the casserole and cook, stirring occasionally, until the meat starts to brown, 10 to 15 minutes. Add the diced carrots and cook until they begin to soften, about 5 minutes.

3) Add the wine, tomato paste, tomatoes with their juices, 1½ cups water, and the bay leaves. Bring to a simmer.

4) Cover and reduce the heat to low. Simmer until the meat is very tender, 2½ to 3 hours. During the last 10 minutes, add the diced celery. Skim off any fat from the surface of the stew. Discard the bay leaves before serving.

Veal Scaloppine
with Prosciutto, Peas, and Artichoke Hearts

V*eal scaloppine are a bonus for home cooks in a hurry because they make elegant meals in a flash.*

Makes 6 servings

2 pounds veal scaloppine,
   pounded thin
½ cup all-purpose flour
2 tablespoons extra-virgin olive
   oil
2 tablespoons butter
3 fresh sage leaves or
   ½ teaspoon dried
¼ teaspoon salt

⅛ teaspoon freshly ground
   pepper
3 tablespoons fresh lemon juice
2 ounces sliced prosciutto or
   ham, cut into thin strips
1 cup frozen peas, thawed
1 (9-ounce) package frozen
   artichoke hearts, thawed

1) Dredge the veal in the flour to coat both sides; shake off any excess. Place the scaloppine on a baking sheet and refrigerate for 20 minutes to set the coating.

2) In a large skillet, heat the olive oil and 1 tablespoon of the butter over medium-high heat. Add the sage leaves, if using. In batches, add the veal and cook until the underside is browned, 2 to 3 minutes. Turn and cook until the other side is browned, about 2 to 3 minutes more. Remove to a platter. Season the veal with the salt and pepper. Add the lemon juice and dried sage, if using, to the skillet and bring to a boil, scraping up the browned bits in the pan with a wooden spoon. Pour over the cutlets and keep warm.

3) Melt the remaining 1 tablespoon butter in the skillet. Add the prosciutto, peas, and artichokes and cook until heated through, about 3 minutes. Pour the prosciutto and vegetables over the veal and serve.

Veal, Red Onion, and Potato Casserole

his casserole is a simple layering of just a few ingredients, but they melt together into a mouthwatering meal-in-a-dish. As an added attraction, the dish can be prepared and refrigerated for up to 8 hours before baking.

Makes 4 to 6 servings

3½ tablespoons extra-virgin olive oil
1 teaspoon dried oregano
½ teaspoon salt
¼ teaspoon freshly ground pepper
1 pound Idaho baking potatoes, peeled and very thinly sliced

2 pounds veal stew meat, trimmed and cut into ½-inch dice
4 medium red onions, thinly sliced
5 ripe plum tomatoes, cut into ¼-inch-thick rounds
1 tablespoon chopped parsley

1) Brush the bottom and sides of a large flameproof casserole with ½ tablespoon of the olive oil. In a small bowl, combine the oregano, salt, and pepper. Add one-third of the potatoes and half of the veal, onions, and tomatoes to the casserole. Sprinkle with one-third of the seasonings and drizzle with 1 tablespoon oil. Repeat the layering, then finish with a layer of potatoes drizzled with the remaining tablespoon oil.

2) Cover tightly with foil and a lid. Cook over low heat, shaking the pan often to be sure the potatoes don't stick, until the potatoes and veal are tender, 1 to 1¼ hours. (If the potatoes seem to be sticking, add a few tablespoons of water to the pot.) Garnish with the parsley and serve from the pot.

Veal Stew with Broccoli and Cauliflower

*T*hese days, most supermarkets sell broccoli and cauliflower florets, so you can buy just the amount you need.

Makes 6 servings

2 garlic cloves, crushed
2 tablespoons extra-virgin olive oil
2½ pounds lean veal stew, cut into 1-inch cubes
1 tablespoon chopped parsley
1 teaspoon chopped fresh sage or ½ teaspoon dried
2 bay leaves

Salt
Freshly ground pepper
½ cup dry white wine
1 (16-ounce) can peeled tomatoes, coarsely chopped, juices reserved
1 cup broccoli florets
1 cup cauliflower florets

1) In a large flameproof casserole, cook the garlic in the olive oil over high heat until it turns golden, about 2 minutes. Discard the garlic. Add the meat in batches and cook, stirring occasionally, until the juices evaporate and the meat browns, about 8 minutes per batch.

2) Return all the meat to the casserole. Add the parsley, sage, bay leaves, ½ teaspoon salt, and ¼ teaspoon pepper. Cook, stirring often, for 2 minutes. Add the wine and cook until it evaporates, 3 to 4 minutes. Stir in the tomatoes with their juices. Cover and reduce the heat to low.

3) Simmer for 1 hour. Alternate the broccoli and cauliflower florets around the outside edge of the casserole and cover. Continue cooking until the vegetables are tender, 10 to 15 minutes. Season with additional salt and pepper to taste. Discard bay leaves and serve.

Veal Stew with Leeks, Carrots, and Brussels Sprouts

Makes 6 to 8 servings

1½ pounds brussels sprouts, trimmed, an "X" cut into each root end

6 medium carrots—3 cut into matchsticks, 3 chopped

2 tablespoons extra-virgin olive oil

4 medium leeks (white parts only), chopped and rinsed

1 medium onion, thinly sliced

5 to 6 pounds veal breast with bones, cut into 1½-inch pieces

½ cup all-purpose flour

1 cup dry white wine

½ teaspoon salt

¼ teaspoon freshly ground pepper

2 teaspoons grainy mustard, such as Pommery

1) In a large Dutch oven, bring 4 quarts of lightly salted water to a boil over high heat. Add the brussels sprouts and cook until almost tender, about 3 minutes. Add the matchstick carrots and continue cooking until both vegetables are tender, about 3 minutes longer. Scoop out 2 cups of the cooking water and set aside. Drain the vegetables, rinse under cold water, and set aside. Wipe the pot dry.

2) In the same pot, heat the olive oil over medium heat. Add the chopped carrots, leeks, and onion. Reduce the heat to medium-low and cover. Cook, stirring occasionally, until the vegetables are softened, 10 to 15 minutes. Increase the heat to medium.

3) Coat the veal in the flour, shaking off any excess. Add to the pot and cook, turning occasionally, until the meat loses its raw look, about 10 minutes. Do not let the meat brown. Add the reserved vegetable liquid, wine, salt, and pepper. Reduce the heat to low and simmer, covered, until the meat is tender, about 1¼ hours.

4) Stir in the reserved vegetables and heat through, 2 to 3 minutes. Just before serving, stir in the mustard.

Veal Stew with Mushrooms and Green Beans

This simple stew combines

some of my homeland's most popular foods—veal, mushrooms, and tomatoes. It also has green beans, and if you can, use the wide, flat broad beans, or pole beans, for real Italian flavor.

Makes 4 to 6 servings

2 tablespoons extra-virgin olive oil
2 pounds lean veal stew, cut into 1½-inch pieces
½ teaspoon salt
¼ teaspoon freshly ground pepper
2 garlic cloves, thinly sliced
½ cup dry white wine

1 pound fresh mushrooms, thinly sliced
2 tablespoons chopped parsley
1 (16-ounce) can peeled tomatoes, coarsely chopped, juices reserved
¾ pound green beans, cut into 2-inch pieces

1) In a large Dutch oven, heat the olive oil over medium-high heat. Add the meat in 2 batches and cook, stirring occasionally, until it is browned on all sides, 6 to 8 minutes per batch. Return all the meat to the pot. Season with the salt and pepper.

2) Add the garlic and cook, stirring often, until fragrant, about 2 minutes. Add the wine and cook until it evaporates, 3 to 4 minutes. Add the mushrooms and 1 tablespoon of the parsley. Cook, stirring occasionally, until the mushrooms are tender and give off their liquid, about 5 minutes. Stir in the chopped tomatoes and cook for 10 minutes. Add the reserved tomato juices and cover.

3) Simmer until the veal is tender, about 45 minutes. Add the green beans and cook 15 minutes longer. Sprinkle with the remaining 1 tablespoon parsley and serve immediately.

Country-Style Osso Buco

Makes 6 servings

½ cup dried porcini mushrooms
2 tablespoons extra-virgin olive oil
1 tablespoon butter
6 veal shanks (5 to 6 pounds), cut into 2-inch-thick pieces
½ cup all-purpose flour
¾ cup dry red wine
½ teaspoon salt
¼ teaspoon freshly ground pepper

3 medium red potatoes, peeled and quartered
2 medium carrots, cut into 1-inch lengths
2 medium celery ribs, cut into 1-inch lengths
1 anchovy fillet packed in oil, minced
1 tablespoon chopped parsley
1 garlic clove, minced
1 teaspoon grated lemon zest

1) In a small bowl, cover the dried mushrooms with 1 cup lukewarm water. Let stand until softened, about 15 minutes. Lift the mushrooms out of the soaking liquid and chop coarsely. Strain the liquid through a paper towel–lined sieve and reserve.

2) In a large Dutch oven, heat the olive oil and butter over medium-high heat. In batches, roll the veal shanks in flour, shaking off the excess, and add to the pot. Cook, turning, until browned on both sides, about 12 minutes. Return all the meat to the pot. Pour in ½ cup wine and let boil until evaporated to about 2 tablespoons, 3 to 4 minutes. Add the chopped mushrooms, ½ cup water, the salt, and the pepper. Reduce the heat to low, cover, and simmer for 1 hour.

3) Add the potatoes, carrots, and celery. Cover and continue cooking until the vegetables and veal are tender, 45 to 60 minutes longer. Use a slotted spoon to remove the veal shanks and vegetables to a platter.

4) Add the remaining ¼ cup wine and ¼ cup water to the pot. Bring to a boil over high heat, scraping up the browned bits from the bottom of the pot. Combine the anchovy fillet, parsley, garlic, and lemon zest. Add to the sauce. Immediately pour the sauce over the veal and vegetables and serve.

Savory Meatballs with Sweet Peppers

T*hese wonderful veal and cheese meatballs in a tangy-sweet pepper and caper sauce are truly out of the ordinary. In America nearly everyone pairs meatballs with spaghetti and tomato sauce, but in Italy we would serve these with mashed potatoes.* **Makes 6 servings**

5 slices of firm-textured white
   bread
⅓ cup milk
¼ cup grated Romano cheese
2 eggs
1½ pounds ground veal or turkey
2 tablespoons chopped parsley
¼ teaspoon salt
¼ teaspoon freshly ground
   pepper

1 cup plain dry bread crumbs
5 tablespoons extra-virgin olive
   oil
4 medium bell peppers,
   preferably 2 red and 2 yellow,
   cut into ½-inch-wide strips
1 garlic clove, minced
2 tablespoons balsamic vinegar
1 tablespoon capers, drained

1) In a medium bowl, soak the bread in the milk until soft, about 5 minutes. Squeeze to remove excess moisture and crumble the bread back into the bowl. Add cheese and eggs and mix well. Add the veal, parsley, salt, and pepper and mix until blended. Using about 3 tablespoons of the mixture for each, form into meatballs. Roll the meatballs in the dry bread crumbs.

2) In a large skillet, heat 3 tablespoons of the olive oil over medium heat. Add the meatballs and cook, turning often, until browned all over, 10 to 15 minutes. Use a slotted spoon to transfer to paper towels to drain.

3) Heat the remaining 2 tablespoons oil in the skillet. Add the bell peppers and garlic. Cook over medium heat, stirring often, until the peppers are softened, about 10 minutes. Stir in the balsamic vinegar and capers. Return the meatballs to the skillet. Cook, uncovered, stirring and turning the meatballs often, 5 minutes longer.

Pork, Sausages, and Lamb

I n Italy, we have always enjoyed all parts of the pig—stews, cutlets, roasts, chops, as well as all sorts of sausages and salamis. Today pork is raised to produce a meat that is not fatty, a boon to those of us who want to eat leaner, but a challenge to the cook who wants to keep meat flavorful and moist. One-pot stews and braises like Neapolitan Medallions of Pork with Sweet Peppers and Mushrooms, Stuffed Pork Palermo Style with Salami and Vegetables, and Sausage and Cabbage Stew provide perfect solutions. Moist-heat cooking keeps the meat tender and juicy while all the added vegetables and aromatics mingle with the pork to produce maximum flavor.

Lamb, too, lends itself beautifully to this type of cooking, and it's a meat with which Italians are most creative. While for flavor and texture I prefer using well-trimmed lamb shoulder for most stews, you can, if you prefer, substitute the leaner meat from the leg. If you do so, reduce the cooking time by about 15 minutes.

The best Italian lamb comes from my region of Abruzzo in the center of Italy, where the sheep graze on the herbs in the mountain meadows in summer, and from the south, where they migrate during the cooler winter months. Consequently, we have a wonderful variety of delicious lamb preparations, with a special fondness for pairing lamb with beans, as in Rosemary Lamb with Balsamic Vinegar and Fava Beans, Leg of Lamb with White Beans and Olives, and Lamb Shanks in Tomato Sauce with Red and White Beans, all of which you'll find here.

Neapolitan Medallions
of Pork with Sweet Peppers
and Mushrooms

*T*hick, center-cut pork loin
*chops are just the thing to simmer in a heady sweet pepper,
mushroom, and garlic sauté. A combination of red, yellow, and
green peppers will give the dish a more complex flavor and
make it look as terrific as it tastes.* ***Makes 6 servings***

¼ cup extra-virgin olive oil
2 garlic cloves, crushed
6 slices of boneless pork loin, cut
  1 inch thick (about 6 ounces
  each)
½ teaspoon salt
¼ teaspoon freshly ground
  pepper

3 medium bell peppers
  (preferably 1 each green, red,
  and yellow), cut into ½-inch-
  wide strips
1 teaspoon chopped fresh
  oregano or ½ teaspoon dried
½ pound fresh mushrooms,
  sliced
1 tablespoon tomato paste

1) In a flameproof Dutch oven, heat 2 tablespoons of the olive oil over medium-high heat. Add 1 garlic clove and cook until sizzling and golden brown, about 2 minutes. Discard the garlic. In 2 batches, cook the pork, turning once, until browned on both sides, 6 to 8 minutes per batch. As they brown, remove the medallions to a plate. Season with salt and pepper.

2) Add the remaining 2 tablespoons oil to the pan and reduce the heat to medium. Add the peppers, oregano, and remaining garlic. Cook, stirring often, until the peppers are tender, about 10 minutes. Add the mushrooms and cook until they soften, about 5 minutes. In a small bowl, dissolve the tomato paste in ¼ cup boiling water. Stir into the pot.

3) Return the pork to the pot and reduce the heat to low. Cover and cook until the medallions are tender with no trace of pink in the center, about 15 minutes. Serve immediately.

Stuffed Pork Palermo Style with Salami and Vegetables

*S*alami mixed with shallots *and rosemary becomes a seasoning for this succulent pork pot roast from Sicily. This is also a great way to prepare a boneless veal shoulder roast.*

Makes 6 servings

2 ounces Genoa salami, finely chopped
2 tablespoons finely chopped shallots or red onion
1 teaspoon chopped fresh rosemary or ½ teaspoon dried
3 pounds boneless pork loin roast
4 tablespoons extra-virgin olive oil

4 medium onions, thinly sliced
3 large red potatoes (about 1¼ pounds), peeled and cut into 1-inch cubes
3 medium carrots, peeled and cut diagonally into 2-inch pieces
1 bay leaf
¼ teaspoon salt
¼ teaspoon freshly ground pepper
1 cup red wine

1) In a small bowl, combine the salami, shallots, and half of the rosemary. Use a small, pointed knife to make slits all over the roast. Fill each slit with some of the salami mixture. Using white kitchen string, tie the roast crosswise and lengthwise.

2) In a large Dutch oven, heat 2 tablespoons of the olive oil over medium-high heat. Add the pork roast and cook, turning occasionally, until browned on all sides, 8 to 10 minutes. Transfer the roast to a platter and set aside. Reduce the heat to medium.

3) Add the remaining 2 tablespoons oil to the Dutch oven and heat. Add the onions and the remaining rosemary. Cook, stirring often, until the onions are golden, about 8 minutes. Add the potatoes, carrots, bay leaf, salt, and pepper. Cook, stirring occasionally, for 3 minutes.

4) Return the roast to the pot and add 1 cup water. Reduce the heat to low, cover, and simmer until the roast is tender, about 1¾ hours. Add ½ cup of the wine and cook, uncovered, until the liquid is almost completely evaporated, about 5 minutes. Remove the roast to a carving board and let stand for about 10 minutes. Meanwhile, use a slotted spoon to remove the vegetables to a serving platter. Discard the bay leaf. Cover loosely with foil to keep warm. Remove the string from the roast and carve the meat crosswise into ½-inch-thick slices. Arrange on the platter with the vegetables.

5) Pour the remaining ½ cup wine and ¼ cup water into the pot and bring to a boil over high heat. Boil, scraping up any browned bits on the bottom and sides of the pot with a wooden spoon, until the sauce is thickened and reduced to about ½ cup, 4 to 6 minutes. Pour the sauce over the meat and vegetables and serve.

Sausages with Broccoli di Rape

This is a simple, classic Italian
method of cooking sausages. No extra oil is needed, and the
broccoli di rape, with its pleasing bite, absorbs some of the flavor
of the meat. All that's needed to accompany this hearty dish is
some good Italian bread and a glass of Chianti. **Makes 6 servings**

2½ pounds sweet Italian
  sausages
1 large bunch of broccoli di rape,
  about 2 pounds

1 garlic clove, minced

1) Pierce each sausage in several places with the tip of a small knife.
Place in a large skillet and add enough water to cover. Cook uncovered
over medium-high heat, turning occasionally, until the water evaporates and
the sausages are nicely browned, about 30 minutes. Remove to a plate.

2) Meanwhile, rinse the broccoli di rape well, but do not dry. Trim off
the rough ends at the bottom and cut the thinner stems and leaves into
1½- to 2-inch lengths.

3) When the sausage is browned, pour off all but 2 tablespoons of the
fat. Add the garlic to the pan and cook until fragrant, about 30 seconds.
Add the broccoli di rape with any water clinging to its leaves and toss to coat
with the juices in the pan. Cover, reduce the heat to medium, and cook,
stirring occasionally, until the broccoli di rape is wilted and just tender, 10 to
12 minutes. If the greens begin to stick, add a few tablespoons of water
to the pan.

4) Cut sausages into 3-inch lengths. Return the sausages to the casserole
along with any juices that have collected on the plate. Toss to mix with
the greens. Cover and cook 5 minutes to reheat the sausages and allow the
flavors to blend.

NOTE: If you use Italian-style turkey or chicken sausages rather than pork
sausages, cover them only halfway with water and cook them 15 to 20
minutes.

Sausage and Cabbage Stew

Makes 6 to 8 servings

1 tablespoon extra-virgin olive
oil
¼ pound pancetta or slab bacon,
rind removed, cut into
¼-inch cubes
2 medium onions, chopped
1½ pounds sweet Italian
sausages, cut into 2-inch
pieces
½ pound thickly sliced boiled
ham, cut into ½-inch cubes
1 small head of cabbage
(1½ pounds), thinly sliced

3 tablespoons red wine vinegar
1 teaspoon sugar
3 cups chicken broth
2 bay leaves
2 teaspoons chopped fresh
thyme or 1 teaspoon dried
8 whole peppercorns
8 juniper berries or 1 tablespoon
gin
6 frankfurters, cut into 2-inch
pieces
1 tablespoon chopped parsley
Boiled potatoes or noodles

1) In a large Dutch oven, heat the olive oil over medium heat. Add the pancetta and cook until lightly browned, about 4 minutes. Add the onions. Cook, stirring often, until the onions are softened and translucent, about 5 minutes. Add the Italian sausage and ham. Cook, stirring often, until the sausage loses its raw look, about 5 minutes longer. Using a slotted spoon, remove the meat and onions to a bowl.

2) Add the cabbage, vinegar, and sugar to the Dutch oven. Cook, stirring often, until the cabbage is wilted, about 5 minutes. Add the broth, bay leaves, thyme, peppercorns, and juniper berries and bring to a simmer. Reduce the heat to low. Cover and cook until the cabbage is tender, about 45 minutes.

3) Return all the meat and onions to the pot. Stir in the frankfurters. Cover and cook until the meats are cooked through, about 15 minutes. Discard the bay leaves. Sprinkle with the parsley and serve with potatoes or noodles.

Sausages with Mushrooms and Onions

My butcher, Louis Arena, not only gives me shopping tips, he occasionally shares a recipe with me, like this simple, delicious sausage dish from his daughter, Debbie. Since I often serve this directly from the skillet, I like to give the skillet a beauty treatment by tying a colorful napkin around the handle before I put it on the table.

Makes 6 to 8 servings

3 pounds sweet Italian sausages
2 medium red onions, sliced
1¼ pounds fresh mushrooms, sliced

4 ripe plum tomatoes, cut into ½-inch dice

1) Pierce each sausage in several places with the tip of a small knife. Place them in a large skillet and add enough water to cover. Cook over medium-high heat, turning occasionally, until the water evaporates and the sausages brown in their own fat, 20 to 30 minutes. Remove to a plate.

2) Pour off all but 2 tablespoons fat from the skillet. Reduce the heat to medium-low. Add the onions and cook, stirring often, until softened and translucent, about 5 minutes. Add the mushrooms. Cover and cook until the mushrooms give off their juices, about 5 minutes. Uncover, increase the heat to medium-high, and cook until the juices evaporate, about 5 minutes. Stir in the tomatoes.

3) Return the sausages to the skillet. Cook, stirring often, until the sausages are reheated, about 5 minutes. Serve immediately.

Cotechino with Lentils

T*his is a Milanese specialty and a very tasty one. The cotechino is an uncooked pork sausage that is available in Italian markets, especially during Christmas. When it is not available, substitute an equal amount of smoked kielbasa. Since the kielbasa is already cooked, add it to the lentils during the last 15 minutes.* **Makes 4 to 6 servings**

1 cotechino, about 2 pounds
2 bay leaves
1 carrot
1 celery rib
1 onion

2 whole cloves
4 to 5 cracked peppercorns
1½ cups lentils, picked over and washed

1) Pierce the cotechino in several places and put it in a soup pot. Add 6 cups water and all the remaining ingredients but the lentils. Cover, bring to a boil, and simmer 30 minutes.

2) Add the lentils and continue cooking 1 hour longer over medium-low heat. Remove the cotechino from the pot, cover with aluminum foil, and set aside. Remove the carrot, celery, and onion from the pot. Place in a food processor and add ¼ cup of the lentils. Puree until smooth. Stir back into the pot. Reheat the lentils until hot.

3) Cut the cotechino into ½-inch slices. Discard the bay leaves, spoon the lentils onto a serving platter, and top with the slices of cotechino.

Braised Lamb with Artichokes and Lemon

At first glance, this would seem to be a stew, but it is actually a spezzatino—a kind of "dry" stew with just enough reduced, intensely flavored sauce to cling to the ingredients. The seasonings here—cinnamon and saffron—were absorbed in Italy from Arab culture, which has mingled with ours since the first century. Serve with rice or mashed potatoes.

Makes 6 servings

2 tablespoons extra-virgin olive oil
3 pounds boneless lamb shoulder, trimmed and cut into 1-inch pieces
½ teaspoon salt
¼ teaspoon freshly ground pepper
¼ cup chicken broth
2 tablespoons fresh lemon juice
½ teaspoon crumbled saffron
½ teaspoon ground cinnamon
1 (9-ounce) package frozen artichoke hearts, thawed
Lemon wedges

1) In a large Dutch oven, heat the olive oil over medium-high heat. Add the lamb in batches without crowding and cook, turning occasionally, until the lamb is browned all over, 6 to 8 minutes. Season the lamb with the salt and pepper. Return all the lamb to the pot.

2) In a small bowl, combine the broth, lemon juice, saffron, and cinnamon. Pour into the Dutch oven. Reduce the heat to low. Simmer, adding water as needed if the juices evaporate, until the meat is tender, about 1 hour. During the last 5 minutes, stir in the artichokes. Serve immediately, with the lemon wedges for garnish, to be squeezed over the stew.

Leg of Lamb with White Beans and Olives

You may cook the lamb here to the degree you prefer, but in Italy it is served rather well done. Look for large, meaty, green olives, preferably from Apulia at Italian grocers' and delicatessens. To pit olives, smash them, one at a time, under a large heavy knife and pick out the pit.

Makes 6 servings

¼ cup all-purpose flour
½ teaspoon salt
¼ teaspoon freshly ground pepper
½ leg of lamb, butt or shank end (2½ to 3 pounds)
3 tablespoons extra-virgin olive oil
1 cup chicken broth
½ teaspoon dried oregano
⅛ teaspoon crushed hot red pepper
2 large carrots, cut into ½-inch dice
1 tablespoon fresh lemon juice
1 (15-ounce) can white beans, preferably cannellini, rinsed and drained
1 cup green olives, pitted

1) In a large shallow dish, combine the flour, salt, and pepper. Dredge the lamb in the seasoned flour to coat; shake off any excess.

2) In a large oval Dutch oven, heat the olive oil over medium-high heat. Add the lamb and cook, turning occasionally, until browned, about 8 minutes. Add ½ cup of the broth, the oregano, and the hot pepper. Cover and reduce the heat to low. Simmer, turning occasionally, for 40 minutes.

3) Add the carrots, lemon juice, and remaining ½ cup broth. Continue cooking until a meat thermometer inserted in the thickest part of the lamb reads 135 degrees F. (for medium lamb), about 50 minutes longer. Transfer to a deep serving platter, leaving the juices in the Dutch oven.

4) Skim off any fat from the surface of the cooking juices. Add the beans and olives. Cook, stirring often, just until heated through, about 5 minutes. Carve the lamb, spoon the bean mixture around the slices, and serve.

Lamb Stew with Fava Beans

M*editerranean cooking wouldn't be the same without fava beans. From Portugal to Turkey, these firm, pale green legumes show up in dish after dish, but I think Italian cooks serve them with special flair. This recipe uses the dried variety, which can be found at Italian grocers'. They need to be soaked overnight and peeled before cooking.*

Makes 4 to 6 servings

2 cups dried fava beans
3 tablespoons extra-virgin olive
 oil
2 ounces pancetta or 2 slices of
 bacon, chopped
2½ pounds boneless leg of lamb,
 trimmed and cut into 1-inch
 pieces
½ teaspoon salt
¼ teaspoon freshly ground
 pepper

1 large onion, sliced
2 garlic cloves, sliced
2 bay leaves
⅛ teaspoon crushed hot red
 pepper
¾ cup dry white wine
1 (28-ounce) can crushed
 tomatoes
1 cup beef or chicken broth
1 tablespoon chopped parsley

1) Place the fava beans in a medium bowl and add enough cold water to cover by 2 inches. Let stand at least 8 hours or overnight; drain. Peel off the tough outer skins. Set the fava beans aside.

2) In a large Dutch oven, heat the olive oil and pancetta over medium heat. Cook, stirring often, until the pancetta is lightly browned, 4 to 5 minutes. Remove the pancetta with a slotted spoon and set aside. Increase the heat to medium-high. In batches without crowding, add the lamb to the Dutch oven and cook, turning occasionally, until the lamb is browned all over, 6 to 8 minutes. As it browns, transfer the lamb to a plate. Season with the salt and pepper.

3) Return all the lamb and the pancetta to the Dutch oven. Add the onion, garlic, bay leaves, and hot pepper. Cook, stirring occasionally, until the onion is softened, about 3 minutes. Add the wine and cook until it evaporates, about 5 minutes. Stir in the tomatoes and ½ cup broth. Cover and reduce the heat to medium-low. Simmer for 30 minutes.

4) Add the fava beans and the remaining ½ cup broth. Cover and simmer until the lamb and beans are tender, about 1 hour longer. Remove and discard the bay leaves. Garnish with the parsley before serving.

Rosemary Lamb with Balsamic Vinegar and Fava Beans

*C*ooking bone-in lamb makes *for delectable eating—ask your butcher to saw the lamb shoulder into 2-inch pieces without removing the bones, which adds extra flavor to the dish. The lamb is marinated overnight, so plan accordingly.*

Makes 6 to 8 servings

5 pounds lamb shoulder with
  bones, trimmed and cut into
  2-inch pieces
1 large onion, chopped
2 medium carrots, chopped
2 medium celery ribs, chopped
1 cup dry white wine
¼ cup extra-virgin olive oil
¼ cup balsamic vinegar
3 sprigs of fresh rosemary or
  1½ teaspoons dried

½ teaspoon salt
¼ teaspoon freshly ground
  pepper
2 cups beef broth
2 cups shelled fresh fava beans
  or 2 (10-ounce) packages
  frozen baby lima beans,
  thawed

1) The day before, combine all of the ingredients except the broth and fava beans in a large bowl and cover tightly. Refrigerate, mixing the ingredients every few hours, for at least 8 hours and up to 24 hours.

2) Preheat the oven to 425 degrees F. Pour the lamb with its marinade and the broth into a large flameproof casserole. Bake uncovered, turning and basting occasionally, until the lamb is tender, 1¼ to 1½ hours. Tilt the pot and skim off any fat from the surface of the cooking liquid.

3) Transfer the pot to the top of the stove. Add the fava beans and simmer until tender, 3 to 5 minutes.

Lamb and Eggplant Casserole

In Abruzzo, where I was born, lamb is king. This simple recipe from my family files uses ground lamb, which I wish were as easy to find as ground beef.
You may have to ask the butcher to grind well-trimmed lamb shoulder or leg for this recipe. Or do it yourself at home in the food processor—buy boneless lamb and freeze the trimmed cubed meat for about 1 hour before processing with the metal blade.

Makes 6 servings

¼ cup extra-virgin olive oil
1 large onion, chopped
1½ pounds lean ground lamb
2 medium eggplants, unpeeled,
   cut into ½-inch cubes
½ teaspoon dried rosemary
¼ teaspoon ground cloves

½ teaspoon salt
¼ teaspoon freshly ground
   pepper
1 teaspoon tomato paste
2 cups tomato puree
¾ cup dried bread crumbs
½ cup grated Romano cheese

1) Preheat the oven to 400 degrees F. In a large flameproof casserole or ovenproof skillet, heat 3 tablespoons of the olive oil over medium heat. Add the onion and cook until softened and translucent, 3 to 5 minutes. Add the ground lamb. Cook, stirring often, until the lamb loses its raw look, about 5 minutes. Tilt the pan to remove all but 2 tablespoons fat.

2) Add the eggplant, rosemary, cloves, salt, and pepper. Cook, stirring often, until the eggplant softens, 8 to 10 minutes. Stir in the tomato paste and tomato puree. Bring to a simmer and cook until slightly thickened, about 5 minutes.

3) In a small bowl, combine the bread crumbs and cheese. Sprinkle over the top of the lamb mixture and drizzle with the remaining 1 tablespoon oil. Bake until the top is golden brown, 15 to 20 minutes. Serve hot.

Lamb with Tiny Onions

In Apulia, where this recipe originated, the lamb would be roasted with lampasciuni, *small onions with a touch of bitterness that add their own special flavor. However, cipolline, small Italian yellow onions available at specialty produce markets and many supermarkets, or even small white boiling onions can be substituted. To loosen their skins for peeling, boil the onions for 1 minute in a large saucepan of boiling water, drain, and rinse.* **Makes 4 to 6 servings**

2½ pounds boneless lamb shoulder, trimmed and cut into 2-inch pieces
2 cups dry white wine
3 tablespoons extra-virgin olive oil
5 ripe plum tomatoes, coarsely chopped
2 garlic cloves, crushed
2 tablespoons chopped parsley

1 tablespoon chopped fresh rosemary or 1 teaspoon dried
½ teaspoon salt
¼ teaspoon freshly ground pepper
1 pound cipolline or white boiling onions, peeled, root ends scored with a shallow "X"
¼ cup dried bread crumbs

1) In a large dish, combine the lamb and wine. Cover and refrigerate for at least 2 hours. Drain, reserving the wine.

2) Preheat the oven to 375 degrees F. Pour 2 tablespoons of the olive oil into a large roasting pan, tilting the pan to coat with oil. Place the lamb in the pan and add the tomatoes, garlic, 1 tablespoon of the parsley, the rosemary, salt, and pepper. Pour in 1 cup of the reserved wine.

3) Bake, basting occasionally with the remaining wine, for 1 hour. Add the cipolline and toss with the pan juices. Bake 30 minutes longer. Sprinkle with the bread crumbs and drizzle with the remaining 1 tablespoon oil. Continue baking until the crumbs are crisp and golden and the meat is tender, 20 to 30 minutes. Sprinkle with the remaining 1 tablespoon parsley and serve immediately.

Braised Lamb Shanks with Carrots and Zucchini

This succulent, satisfying dish is a cinch to prepare, but you must allow plenty of time for the shanks to simmer to melting tenderness. Lamb shanks can weigh up to 1½ pounds. Shanks weighing about 1 pound each are perfect for individual servings; adjust the cooking time accordingly for larger ones.

Makes 4 servings

3 tablespoons extra-virgin olive oil
4 medium lamb shanks (about 1 pound each)
½ teaspoon salt
¼ teaspoon freshly ground pepper
2 large onions, chopped
1 medium celery rib, chopped
1 garlic clove, minced
2 tablespoons chopped parsley
1½ cups dry red wine
2 cups chicken broth
2 bay leaves
3 medium carrots, sliced into ½-inch-thick rounds
3 medium zucchini, cut into 1-inch pieces

1) In a large skillet or Dutch oven, heat the olive oil over medium-high heat. Add the shanks, in batches if necessary, and cook, turning occasionally, until browned all over, 6 to 8 minutes. Season the lamb shanks with the salt and pepper. Add the onions, celery, garlic, and 1 tablespoon of the parsley. Cook, stirring occasionally, until the vegetables are soft, about 3 minutes.

2) Add the wine and cook until the wine is evaporated, 8 to 10 minutes. Add 1 cup broth and the bay leaves. Cover and reduce the heat to medium-low. Simmer for 1 hour.

3) Add the remaining 1 cup broth and simmer, covered, 45 minutes longer. Add the carrots and zucchini and simmer about 15 minutes. Remove and discard the bay leaves. Sprinkle with the remaining 1 tablespoon parsley before serving.

Lamb Shanks in Tomato Sauce
with Red and White Beans

L*amb shanks, simmered in a gusty tomato and red wine sauce until the meat falls off the bone, is a grand dish for a cool evening. Using red and white beans gives this homey dish a festive look.* ***Makes 4 servings***

3 tablespoons extra-virgin olive
  oil
4 medium lamb shanks
½ teaspoon salt
¼ teaspoon freshly ground pepper
2 garlic cloves, crushed
1 large onion, sliced
2 medium carrots, chopped
2 medium celery ribs, chopped
1 large sprig of fresh rosemary or
  1 teaspoon dried

1 cup dry red wine
1 (28-ounce) can peeled tomatoes,
  juices reserved
4 cups chicken broth
1 tablespoon tomato paste
2 bay leaves
1 (15-ounce) can white beans,
  preferably cannellini, rinsed
  and drained
1 (15-ounce) can red kidney
  beans, rinsed and drained

1) In a large, deep skillet or saucepan, heat the olive oil over medium-high heat. Add the lamb, in batches if necessary, and cook, turning occasionally, until browned all over, 6 to 8 minutes. Season the lamb shanks with the salt and pepper. Return all the meat to the skillet.

2) Add the garlic and cook until fragrant, about 1 minute. Add the onion, carrots, celery, and rosemary. Cook, stirring often, until the onion softens, 3 to 5 minutes. Add the wine, bring to a boil, and cook until it almost completely evaporates. Add the tomatoes with their juices, broth, tomato paste, and bay leaves. Bring to a simmer and reduce the heat to medium-low. Cover and simmer until the meat is very tender, about 2 hours. Skim off any fat from the surface of the cooking liquid.

3) Stir in the beans. Simmer until the beans are heated through, about 5 minutes. Remove and discard the rosemary sprig and bay leaves before serving.

Seafood Mediterraneo

Surrounded as it is on three sides by the sea, Italy is a paradise for seafood lovers. Not counting the so-called *brodetti,* or fish stews, which are indigenous to every village and town along the coastline, every region has its own specialty. The recipes are as varied as the landscape and are often tailored to the special fish that is being cooked.

Apart from large tuna and swordfish, which swim in the Mediterranean and are principally the domain of the Sicilians, our fish are usually small, and for this reason we believe in cooking them on the bone and with the head on; that way, much flavor is retained. However, I know that many Americans find this upsetting and that whole fish are harder to find, so in this chapter, I have called for only fish fillets and steaks, as well as all manner of shellfish: shrimp, scallops, mussels, clams, lobster, and squid.

All of my recipes give you a range of cooking times, but to keep fish moist and tender, it is especially important to pay attention, since thickness of the fish and stove heats can vary and just a couple of minutes can make a big difference. To see if your fish is done, stick a thin knife in the thickest part of the fillet or steak, pry it open slightly, and see if the flesh has lost its raw look and has started to turn opaque, that is, white rather than translucent, in the center.

From north to south, even from Naples to Sicily, types of fish and flavorings vary. Though the styles of cooking seafood and the basic flavorings are classic, where necessary I have substituted fish that is widely available in the United States. That way, I hope you'll enjoy the full range of seafood in this chapter, from the subtle and elegant Baked Red Snapper with Cremini Mushrooms and Baked Sole Stuffed with Shrimp to the heartier, tangy Swordfish Sicilian Style and Seafood and Potato Stew with Garlic Sauce.

Baked Red Snapper with Cremini Mushrooms

*C*remini mushrooms, those *full-flavored, brownish mushrooms found in practically every supermarket, bring a touch of Italy to the local produce department. If you can't find them, use ordinary white button mushrooms. Serve this dish with rice.* ***Makes 6 servings***

¼ cup olive oil
6 red snapper fillets (2½ to 3 pounds)
½ pound thinly sliced cremini mushrooms
3 leeks (white and tender green), well rinsed and sliced into very thin rounds

2 tablespoons chopped fresh parsley
2 garlic cloves, finely chopped
¼ teaspoon salt
¼ teaspoon freshly ground pepper
½ cup dry white wine
1 tablespoon fresh lemon juice

1) Preheat the oven to 375 degrees F. Lightly oil a large baking dish. Arrange the fish in the dish, alternating the wide and thin ends of the fillets from right to left, so the fish will fit in a single layer. Sprinkle with the mushrooms and leeks, then the parsley and garlic. Season with the salt and pepper. Drizzle with the remaining olive oil.

2) Bake for 20 minutes. Add the wine and continue baking, basting occasionally, 15 minutes longer. Drizzle with the lemon juice and serve.

Poached Sea Bass and Leeks in Roasted Red Pepper Sauce

I *always have a jar of red peppers in my cupboard. In a flash, they are turned into a creamy, elegant, rose-colored sauce for fish fillets. Serve with steamed rice.*

Makes 6 servings

6 medium leeks (white and
   tender green), split
   lengthwise in half and well
   rinsed
¼ teaspoon freshly ground
   pepper
1 cup dry white wine
½ cup fish broth or ¼ cup bottled
   clam juice mixed with ¼ cup
   water

2 (7-ounce) jars roasted red
   peppers, drained, and rinsed
¼ cup heavy cream
Salt
6 striped bass fillets (about
   2½ pounds)

1) Place the leeks in a shallow, flameproof casserole and season with the pepper. Pour in the wine, broth, and ½ cup water. Bring to a simmer over high heat. Reduce the heat to medium-low. Cover and simmer until the leeks are just tender, 10 to 15 minutes.

2) Meanwhile, in a blender or food processor, puree the red peppers and cream. Season with salt to taste. Set aside.

3) Arrange the fish fillets over the leeks and baste with the pan juices. Cover again and cook over medium heat until the fish flakes, 5 to 8 minutes. Spoon the sauce over the fillets and serve.

Steamed Cod and Potatoes with Saffron-Basil Sauce

O*range juice is an interesting change from the usual lemon juice found in fish dishes, and with saffron and basil, it is an intriguing blend, indeed. Just about any white-fleshed fish steaks or fillets can be prepared this way. Try it cold, with a dollop of mayonnaise topping each serving.*

Makes 4 servings

1 pound small red potatoes, scrubbed and quartered
1¼ cups fish broth or ¾ cup bottled clam juice mixed with ½ cup water
1 cup dry white wine
½ cup orange juice, preferably fresh
3 tablespoons finely chopped shallots

2 garlic cloves, minced
½ teaspoon powdered saffron
1 bay leaf
4 cod or scrod steaks (½ pound each)
¼ teaspoon salt
¼ teaspoon freshly ground pepper
2 tablespoons chopped basil
1 teaspoon chopped parsley

1) In a large skillet or flameproof casserole, cover the potatoes with lightly salted water and bring to a boil over high heat. Reduce the heat to medium. Cook the potatoes for 5 minutes. Drain and return the potatoes to the skillet.

2) Add the broth, wine, orange juice, shallots, half the garlic, the saffron, and bay leaf. Bring to a simmer, cover, reduce the heat to medium-low, and cook until the potatoes are just tender, about 15 minutes.

3) Arrange the fish over the potatoes and season with the salt and pepper. Cover and cook until the potatoes are tender and the fish flakes easily, about 3 to 5 minutes longer. Remove and discard the bay leaf. Sprinkle with the basil, parsley, and remaining garlic. Spoon the fish, potatoes, and juices into individual soup bowls and serve.

Ragout of Haddock with Summer Vegetables

For years, Italian cooks thought that corn, outside of being ground into polenta, was only fit for the farm trough. Finally it is being appreciated for its sweet goodness. I had a dish like this at a trattoria on the Adriatic coast—fish steaks cooked on top of an irresistible mix of summer vegetables, accented with golden corn. **Makes 6 servings**

3 tablespoons extra-virgin olive oil
1 large onion, chopped
4 Italian frying peppers, cut into 1-inch squares, or use 2 bell peppers, preferably 1 red and 1 green
2 garlic cloves, finely chopped
2 small zucchini, cut into ½-inch dice
2½ pounds haddock or cod fillets, cut into 1½-inch cubes

2 cups fresh or frozen corn kernels
3 ripe plum tomatoes, cut into ¼-inch dice
1 tablespoon chopped fresh basil
¼ teaspoon salt
¼ teaspoon freshly ground pepper
1 tablespoon chopped parsley

1) In a large skillet, heat the olive oil over medium heat. Add the onion, peppers, and garlic and cook, stirring often, until softened, about 7 minutes. Add the zucchini and cook, stirring often, until crisp-tender, 3 to 5 minutes. Stir in the fish, corn, tomatoes, basil, salt, and pepper.

2) Cover and reduce the heat to medium-low. Cook, shaking the pan occasionally, until the fish is opaque, about 5 minutes. Sprinkle with the parsley and serve.

Monkfish in Genovese Mushroom Sauce

In the trattorie *around Genoa's famed seaport, you will find this assertive, delicious stew often served with rice or even pasta.* **Makes 6 servings**

¼ cup dried porcini mushrooms

3 tablespoons extra-virgin olive oil

1 medium onion, chopped

6 anchovy fillets in oil, finely chopped

12 ounces fresh mushrooms, thinly sliced

2 garlic cloves, finely chopped

2 tablespoons chopped parsley

¼ teaspoon freshly ground pepper

½ cup dry white wine

1 tablespoon tomato paste

3 pounds monkfish, cut into 6 equal pieces

1) In a small bowl, cover the dried mushrooms with ½ cup warm water. Let stand until softened, about 15 minutes. Lift the mushrooms out of the soaking liquid and chop coarsely. Strain the liquid through a paper towel–lined sieve and reserve.

2) In a large skillet, heat the olive oil over medium heat. Add the onion and cook, stirring often, until softened and translucent, 3 to 5 minutes. Add the anchovies and stir until they have dissolved into the onions, about 2 minutes. Add the fresh mushrooms, soaked mushrooms, garlic, 1 tablespoon parsley, and pepper. Cover and cook until the mushrooms give off their liquid, about 10 minutes.

3) Stir in the wine and increase the heat to high. Boil until the wine evaporates almost completely, about 10 minutes. Add the mushroom soaking liquid and tomato paste and bring to a boil, stirring to dissolve the tomato paste. Reduce the heat to medium and simmer until the liquid is reduced by half, about 5 minutes. Add the fish and cover.

4) Cook until the fish flakes easily, 8 to 10 minutes. Sprinkle with the remaining 1 tablespoon parsley and serve.

Salmon with Artichokes and Potatoes

Artichokes and potatoes are *beautiful together. Topped with pink salmon, this is a lovely dish for a spring supper.*   ***Makes 4 servings***

2 tablespoons butter
1 medium onion, chopped
1 (9-ounce) package frozen artichoke hearts, thawed
2 tablespoons extra-virgin olive oil
2 medium red potatoes, peeled and thinly sliced
⅓ cup all-purpose flour

¼ teaspoon salt
¼ teaspoon freshly ground pepper
4 salmon steaks (6 to 8 ounces each)
1 tablespoon finely chopped chives or scallions
Lemon wedges

1) In a large skillet, heat 1 tablespoon of the butter over medium heat. Add the onion and cook, stirring often, until softened and translucent, 3 to 5 minutes. Add the artichokes and cook until heated through, about 5 minutes. Remove to a bowl and set aside.

2) In the same skillet, heat the remaining 1 tablespoon butter and 1 tablespoon of the olive oil. Add the potatoes and cook, turning often, until tender, about 15 minutes. Add to the artichokes.

3) Add the remaining 1 tablespoon oil to the skillet and heat. In a shallow dish, combine the flour, salt, and pepper. Coat the salmon with the seasoned flour; shake off any excess. Place in the skillet and cook over medium heat, turning once, until lightly browned outside and just barely opaque in the center, 5 to 7 minutes. Remove to a platter.

4) Return the potatoes, onion, and artichokes to the skillet. Cook over high heat, tossing, until reheated, 1 to 2 minutes. Spoon around the salmon and sprinkle with the chives. Garnish with the lemon wedges and serve at once.

Salt Cod alla Vicentina

Mediterranean cooks love
salt cod and have many interesting preparations for this
humble food. However, baccalà, as it is called in Italy, is no longer
considered just peasant food. This dish with its creamy sauce,
a specialty of Vicenza, is served in some very elegant ristoranti,
always with golden polenta. Note that the cod is soaked in
several changes of cold water in the refrigerator for at least 3 days
to remove excess salt before making the dish.   ***Makes 6 servings***

2 pounds salt cod
3 tablespoons extra-virgin olive
   oil
2 large onions, chopped
2 tablespoons flour
2 anchovies packed in oil,
   drained and chopped

2 tablespoons chopped fresh
   parsley
¼ teaspoon freshly ground
   pepper
2 cups hot milk
2 tablespoons grated Parmesan
   cheese

1) In a large bowl, cover the salt cod with cold water. Refrigerate,
changing the water every 8 hours, for 3 to 4 days. Drain the salt cod.
Remove the skin and pick out any bones.

2) Preheat the oven to 325 degrees F. In a shallow flameproof casserole,
heat the olive oil over medium heat. Add the onions and cook, stirring
often, until golden, about 8 minutes. Sprinkle on the flour and add
the anchovies, parsley, and pepper. Cook, stirring, about 1 minute. Remove
from the heat. Arrange the fish in the casserole and pour in the hot milk.
Sprinkle with the Parmesan cheese.

3) Bake uncovered until the salt cod has absorbed the milk, 30 to
40 minutes.

Baked Sole Stuffed with Shrimp

Stuffed fish fillets abound *throughout the Mediterranean. This version gets Italian flair with a bit of Parmesan cheese and garlic.* **Makes 6 servings**

½ pounds large shrimp, peeled, deveined, and coarsely chopped
¼ cup bread crumbs
1 egg, beaten
1 tablespoon grated Parmesan cheese
2 tablespoons chopped parsley
½ teaspoon chopped fresh sage or ¼ teaspoon dried
⅛ teaspoon salt

⅛ teaspoon freshly ground pepper
1 tablespoon extra-virgin olive oil
1 garlic clove, thinly sliced
12 small sole or flounder fillets (3 to 4 ounces each)
3 tablespoons butter, cut into small pieces
⅓ cup dry white wine

1) Preheat the oven to 350 degrees F. In a medium bowl, mix the shrimp, 2 tablespoons of the bread crumbs, the egg, Parmesan cheese, 1 tablespoon of the parsley, the sage, salt, and pepper.

2) Spread the olive oil over the bottom of a 9 × 13-inch baking dish. Scatter the garlic over the bottom of the dish. Place 6 fillets in the dish. Spread the shrimp filling evenly over the fillets and dot with 1½ tablespoons of the butter. Cover the filling with the 6 remaining fillets. Combine the remaining 2 tablespoons bread crumbs and 1 tablespoon parsley and sprinkle on top. Dot with the remaining butter. Pour the wine around the fillets.

3) Bake, basting occasionally, until the crumbs are golden brown and the fish is opaque in the center, about 20 minutes.

Swordfish Sicilian Style

*S*icilians love to mix many different flavors and textures in the same dish. Take this one—sweet raisins, pungent capers, salty olives, smooth melted cheese, tangy tomatoes, and briny swordfish. Centuries of fine cooking have proven this mélange to be very harmonious and not in the least discordant. Caciocavallo cheese can be found at Italian grocers, or use provolone. **Makes 6 servings**

½ cup flour
¼ teaspoon salt
¼ teaspoon freshly ground pepper
6 slices of swordfish, cut ½ inch thick (about 3 pounds)
⅓ cup extra-virgin olive oil
1 medium onion, chopped
1 medium carrot, chopped
1 medium celery rib, chopped
4 ripe medium tomatoes, peeled, seeded, and chopped

2 tablespoons chopped basil
1 tablespoon chopped parsley
½ cup black Mediterranean olives, pitted and coarsely chopped
1 tablespoon capers
1 tablespoon raisins
½ cup shredded caciocavallo or provolone cheese

1) In a shallow dish, combine the flour, salt, and pepper. Dredge the fish in the seasoned flour; shake off any excess. In a large skillet, heat ¼ cup of the olive oil over medium-high heat. Add the fish to the skillet and cook, turning once, until browned on both sides, about 5 minutes. Remove to a plate and set aside. Discard any oil in the skillet.

2) In the same skillet, heat the remaining olive oil over medium-low heat. Add the onion, carrot, and celery. Cook, stirring often, until the vegetables are softened, about 10 minutes. Add the tomatoes, basil, and parsley. Cook, stirring occasionally, until the tomato juices thicken, about 20 minutes. Stir in the olives, capers, and raisins.

3) Return the swordfish to the skillet and sprinkle with the cheese. Simmer until the cheese has melted, about 5 minutes.

Trout with Porcini and Bread Stuffing and Roasted Asparagus

Porcini mushrooms combined
*with bread crumbs make a superb filling for fish. In Italy, this
stuffing is usually used for fresh sardines, but here it works very
well with rainbow trout. I use a 14-inch paella pan to bake the
fish in a spoke pattern, or arrange it in rows in a large baking dish.*

Makes 6 servings

½ cup dried porcini mushrooms
1½ cups (½-inch) cubed stale
  Italian bread
¼ cup milk
1 egg, beaten
2 tablespoons grated Parmesan
  cheese
½ teaspoon dried marjoram or
  oregano
¼ teaspoon grated nutmeg
¼ teaspoon salt

⅛ teaspoon freshly ground
  pepper
6 whole trout (8 ounces each),
  boned
3 tablespoons bread crumbs
2½ tablespoons extra-virgin
  olive oil
2 pounds fresh asparagus, tough
  ends removed
Lemon wedges

1) In a small bowl, cover the dried mushrooms with ¾ cup warm water.
Let stand until softened, about 15 minutes. Lift the mushrooms out of the
soaking liquid and chop coarsely. Strain the liquid through a paper
towel–lined sieve and reserve for another use.

2) In a medium bowl, soak the bread cubes in the milk, stirring often,
until softened, about 5 minutes. Squeeze the milk out of the bread and
return the bread to the bowl. Add the chopped mushrooms, egg, Parmesan
cheese, marjoram, nutmeg, salt, and pepper and blend well. Stuff each
trout with some of the mixture, reserving any extra filling.

3) Spoke-fashion, place the fish in a lightly oiled large, round baking
dish or paella pan, or use 1 or 2 rectangular baking dishes and arrange

fish in rows. Season lightly with additional salt and pepper. Sprinkle with the bread crumbs and any leftover filling. Drizzle 1 tablespoon of the olive oil over the crumbs. Toss the asparagus with the remaining 1½ tablespoons of oil and arrange in small bundles between the fish.

4) Bake until the fish is opaque, the crumbs are golden brown, and the asparagus is just tender, 30 to 40 minutes. Serve with lemon wedges.

Seafood and Potato Stew with Garlic Sauce

This dish, redolent with garlic, can be traced back to the Phoenicians. Wherever they traded, from Sicily to the Riviera (and west of France, where it became bourride), they inspired the local cooks to try their hands at this thick, hearty fish stew.   **Makes 8 servings**

1 pound large shrimp, peeled and deveined, shells reserved

¼ cup extra-virgin olive oil

1 medium onion, chopped

1 medium leek (white and tender green), well rinsed and chopped

1 medium carrot, chopped

2 bay leaves

1 cup dry white wine

2 (2-inch) strips of orange zest, removed with a vegetable peeler

1½ cups canned crushed tomatoes

3 large red potatoes, cut into 1-inch cubes

½ pound squid, cleaned, tentacles cut off and reserved, sacs cut into ½-inch-thick rings

2 pounds cod fillets, cut into 1½-inch cubes

1 pound monkfish fillets, cut into 1½-inch cubes

Salt and freshly ground pepper

1 hard-cooked egg

3 garlic cloves, crushed through a press

1 tablespoon chopped parsley

8 slices of Italian bread, toasted

1) Wrap the shrimp shells in a large piece of cheesecloth, tie with kitchen string, and set aside. In a large nonreactive stew pot, heat 2 tablespoons of the olive oil over medium-low heat. Add the onion, leek, carrot, and bay leaves. Cook, stirring often, until the onion is tender, 5 to 8 minutes. Add 4 cups water, the shells in the cheesecloth, wine, and orange zest. Bring to a boil over high heat. Return the heat to medium-low and simmer for 15 minutes. Add the tomatoes and simmer 10 to 15 minutes.

Remove the cheesecloth bundle, squeezing the liquid back into the pot, and discard.

2) Layer the potatoes in the pot and top with the squid tentacles and rings. Cover and simmer for 40 minutes. Add the cod and monkfish and simmer for 10 minutes. Add the shrimp and cook until they turn firm and bright pink, about 3 minutes. Season with salt and pepper to taste.

3) Meanwhile, in a small bowl, use a fork to mash the hard-cooked egg, garlic, and parsley. Gradually work in the remaining 2 tablespoons oil to make a smooth paste. (Or process in a mini-food processor.) Place in a small serving bowl.

4) Remove and discard bay leaves. Spoon the stew into deep soup bowls. Serve with the toasted bread and garlic sauce, letting each guest spread the sauce on the bread to dip into the soup.

Fish Steaks Livornese

T*he Livornese make this dish with small, whole mullets from the Tuscan coastline, but it is just as delicious with thick steaks of firm, white-fleshed fish like cod or haddock.*   ***Makes 4 servings***

2 tablespoons extra-virgin olive oil
3 garlic cloves, finely chopped
1 teaspoon finely chopped fresh sage or ½ teaspoon dried
1 (28-ounce) can peeled tomatoes, coarsely chopped, juices reserved

4 cod, scrod, or haddock steaks (½ pound each)
¼ teaspoon salt
¼ teaspoon freshly ground pepper
1½ cups fresh or frozen peas
1 tablespoon chopped parsley

1) In a large skillet, heat the olive oil over medium heat. Add the garlic and sage. Stir until the garlic turns golden, about 1 minute. Add the tomatoes with ½ cup of the reserved juices and bring to a simmer. Cook until the sauce thickens slightly, about 10 minutes.

2) Add the fish, salt, and pepper. Cover and cook for 5 minutes. Add the peas and continue cooking until the fish flakes easily, 3 to 5 minutes. Sprinkle with the parsley and serve.

Venetian Brodetto of Seafood

*B*rodetto is not a soup, as the Italian name may suggest; it is a casserole in which an assortment of fish and shellfish are cooked in a sauce. This is a Venetian specialty. Serve with thick slices of crusty Italian bread, toasted and brushed with olive oil, or with polenta.

Makes 6 servings

¼ cup extra-virgin olive oil
1 medium onion, thinly sliced
3 garlic cloves, minced
2 tablespoons chopped parsley
¼ teaspoon powdered saffron
½ pound cleaned squid, tentacles cut off and reserved, squid cut into ½-inch-thick rings
¼ cup red wine vinegar
1 teaspoon tomato paste

1 (14½-ounce) can diced peeled tomatoes, juices reserved
1 pound firm, white-fleshed fish fillets, cut into 1½-inch cubes
1½ pounds monkfish fillets, cut into 1½-inch cubes
½ pounds large shrimp, peeled and deveined
12 littleneck clams or mussels, scrubbed

1) In a large nonreactive flameproof casserole with a lid, heat the olive oil over medium heat. Add the onion, garlic, 1 tablespoon of the parsley, and the saffron. Cook, stirring often, until the onion is softened and translucent, 3 to 5 minutes.

2) Add the squid, cover, and cook over low heat for 10 minutes. Stir in ¼ cup water, the vinegar, and the tomato paste. Bring to a simmer, stirring to dissolve the tomato paste. Cook, covered, for 5 minutes. Add the tomatoes and their juices, cover, and cook for 10 minutes.

3) Add the fish and monkfish, cover, and cook for 5 minutes. Add the shrimp and clams. Cover and cook until the clams have opened, about 5 minutes. Sprinkle with the remaining parsley and serve at once in deep soup bowls.

Baked Lobster Casserole

T*his is a luxurious dish, making up in ease what it lacks in thrift. Boil two lobsters and shell them yourself, or purchase shelled lobster meat from the best fish store in town.*　　　　　*Makes 4 servings*

2 tablespoons butter
1 tablespoons extra-virgin olive
　oil
1 small onion, finely chopped
2½ cups shelled cooked lobster
　meat, cut into 1-inch pieces
2 tablespoons dry Marsala or
　sherry

½ cup heavy cream
1 (9-ounce) package frozen
　artichoke hearts, thawed
2 tablespoons dried bread
　crumbs
1 tablespoon chopped parsley
1 tablespoon grated Parmesan
　cheese

1) Preheat the oven to 400 degrees F. In a medium shallow, flameproof casserole, heat 1 tablespoon of the butter and the olive oil over medium heat. Add the onion, and cook, stirring often, until the onion is softened, about 3 minutes. Add the Marsala and cook until it evaporates, 2 to 3 minutes.

2) Stir in the lobster and cream; distribute the artichokes on top. Combine the bread crumbs, parsley, and Parmesan and sprinkle over all. Dot with the remaining 1 tablespoon butter.

3) Bake until the casserole is bubbling and the top is golden brown, 10 to 15 minutes.

Mussels with White Beans

*C*hef Paul Bartollotta of
Chicago's Spiaggia restaurant shared this simple recipe with me.
The combination of shellfish and beans is classically Italian. Serve
with slices of bruschetta, grilled or toasted Italian bread
brushed with olive oil and rubbed with garlic.

Makes 4 to 6 servings

3 tablespoons extra-virgin olive
  oil
1 tablespoon butter
1 garlic clove, minced
4 pounds mussels, scrubbed and
  debearded
1½ cups dry white wine
¼ teaspoon crushed hot pepper
  flakes

1 (19-ounce) can cannellini
  beans, rinsed and drained
6 ripe plum tomatoes, seeded
  and cut into ½-inch dice
3 tablespoons chopped parsley
Salt

1) In a large soup pot, heat 2 tablespoons of the olive oil and the butter
over medium heat. Add the garlic and cook, stirring, until it begins to
color, 1 to 2 minutes. Add the mussels, wine, and hot pepper. Cover and
increase the heat to high. Cook until the mussels have opened, 4 to 5
minutes. Use a slotted spoon or tongs to remove the mussels to a large bowl.
Discard any mussels that do not open. Strain the cooking liquid through
a paper towel–lined sieve into a bowl. Working over the bowl to collect the
juices, shell the mussels; discard the shells. Rinse the pot. Strain the
juices back into the pot.

2) Add 2½ cups water and the remaining 1 tablespoon oil. Bring to
a simmer over medium heat. Add the beans and tomatoes and cook until
they are heated through, 3 to 5 minutes. Stir in the shelled mussels
and parsley and simmer for 1 minute. Season with salt to taste. Ladle into
bowls to serve.

Mussels in Creamy Sauce

My friend Lidia Bastianich *can cook plain or fancy, extravagant or homey, and the food is always exceptional and delicious. The home version of her sauce for this stew is so rich you'll suspect it's laden with cream, but it's just milk. Serve it with crusty bread for sopping up the juices to your heart's content.* **Makes 4 servings**

3 tablespoons extra-virgin olive oil
2 medium onions, thinly sliced
2 garlic cloves, thinly sliced
1 cup dry white wine
4 pounds mussels, scrubbed and debearded

1 tablespoon butter
1 teaspoon flour
½ cup milk
1 tablespoon finely chopped parsley

1) In a large Dutch oven or pot, heat the olive oil over medium heat. Add the onions and garlic. Cook, stirring often and gradually adding ½ cup of the wine, until the onions are quite soft and the wine has evaporated, 5 to 7 minutes.

2) Add the mussels and the remaining ½ cup wine. Cover and increase the heat to high. Cook until all the mussels have opened, 5 to 7 minutes. Use a slotted spoon or tongs to remove the mussels to a large bowl as soon as they open. Loosely cover with foil to keep warm. Discard any that do not open. Strain the cooking liquid through a paper towel–lined sieve into a small bowl. Wipe the pot clean with paper towels.

3) In the same pot, melt the butter over medium heat. Sprinkle in the flour and cook, stirring constantly to prevent browning, for 1 minute. Whisk in the reserved cooking liquid from the mussels and the milk. Bring just to a boil, whisking until smooth. Divide the mussels among deep soup bowls and ladle the sauce over them. Garnish with parsley and serve.

Scallop and Pesto Stew

Tasty, colorful, easy—this dish has a lot to offer. Smaller bay scallops cook quickly, so keep an eye on them lest they overcook and toughen. If using the larger sea scallops, cut them into halves or even quarters to make ¾-inch cubes. Shredded radicchio leaves make an unusual garnish and offer a slightly bitter contrast to the sweet scallops. Serve with crusty Italian bread.

Makes 4 servings

1½ cups loosely packed fresh
   basil leaves
1 sprig of parsley, with stem
2 garlic cloves, smashed
5 tablespoons extra-virgin olive
   oil
2 medium zucchini, cut into
   ½-inch dice
3 ripe medium tomatoes, peeled,
   seeded, and cut into ½-inch
   dice

¼ teaspoon salt
⅛ teaspoon freshly ground
   pepper
1½ pounds bay scallops
3 radicchio leaves, thinly
   shredded

1) In a blender or food processor, combine the basil, parsley, garlic, and 3 tablespoons of the olive oil. Puree until fairly smooth. Remove the pesto to a bowl and set aside.

2) In a large skillet, heat the remaining 2 tablespoons oil over medium-high heat. Add the zucchini and cook, stirring occasionally, until lightly browned, 5 to 7 minutes. Stir in the tomatoes, salt, and pepper and bring to a simmer. Reduce the heat to medium and cook, stirring occasionally, until the tomatoes give off their juices and they begin to thicken, about 5 minutes.

3) Stir in 1 tablespoon of the pesto and add the scallops. Cook, stirring occasionally, until they turn opaque, 3 to 5 minutes. Spoon into soup bowls, topping each serving with a dollop of the remaining pesto and some shredded radicchio.

Shrimp, Scallop, and Mushroom Gratin

Fish and cheese is an absolute *no-no in Italy, but as usual there are exceptions. If the dish does not contain oil or tomato and is cooked with some cream or milk, cheese is not only allowed, but is a must.*   ***Makes 4 servings***

3 tablespoons unsalted butter
¼ pound fresh mushrooms, sliced
1 teaspoon chopped fresh sage or ¼ teaspoon dried
¼ teaspoon grated nutmeg
1½ pounds large shrimp, peeled and deveined
½ pound bay scallops

4 ounces smoked mozzarella cheese, cut into ¼-inch dice
½ cup heavy cream
¼ cup grated Parmesan cheese
⅛ teaspoon salt
⅛ teaspoon freshly ground pepper
2 tablespoons dried bread crumbs

1) Preheat the oven to 375 degrees F. In a large oval gratin dish, melt 2 tablespoons of the butter over medium heat. Add the mushrooms, sage, and nutmeg. Cook the mushrooms, stirring occasionally, until they give off their liquid. Let the liquid evaporate and cook until the mushrooms begin to brown, about 8 minutes. Remove to a medium mixing bowl.

2) Add the shrimp, scallops, mozzarella cheese, cream, Parmesan cheese, salt, and pepper to the mushrooms and mix well. Place the mixture in the gratin dish and smooth the top to even. Sprinkle with the bread crumbs and dot with the remaining 1 tablespoon butter.

3) Bake until bubbling and golden brown, 20 to 25 minutes.

Squid with Red Peppers and Broccoli *in Padella*

W*hen in Beijing, call it a stir-fry. When in Rome, call it* in padella. *This dish may seem like a Chinese-Italian hybrid, but ginger has been around our kitchens since the Renaissance era. Balsamic vinegar gives the dish definitive Italian gusto.*

Makes 4 to 6 servings

¼ cup extra-virgin olive oil
2 pounds squid, cleaned, tentacles cut off and coarsely chopped, squid cut into ½-inch-wide rings
1 tablespoon grated fresh ginger
2 garlic cloves, sliced
1 tablespoon dry sherry

3 red peppers, cut into ½-inch-wide strips
2 cups broccoli florets
5 scallions, finely chopped
1 tablespoon balsamic vinegar
¼ teaspoon salt
¼ teaspoon freshly ground pepper

1) In a large skillet, heat 2 tablespoons of the olive oil over medium-high heat. Add the squid, ginger, and garlic. Cook, stirring almost constantly, until the squid is almost tender, 1 to 2 minutes. Add the sherry and stir for 1 minute. Remove the squid to a bowl.

2) Heat the remaining 2 tablespoons oil in the skillet. Add the peppers and cook over medium heat, stirring often, until tender, about 10 minutes. Pour into the bowl with the squid.

3) Add the broccoli and ⅓ cup water to the skillet. Cover and cook for about 5 minutes. Stir in the scallions, cover, and cook until the broccoli is crisp-tender, 1 to 2 minutes longer.

4) Return the squid and peppers to the skillet and stir until heated through, about 2 minutes. Stir in the vinegar, salt, and pepper and serve.

NOTE: Squid is either cooked very briefly, as in this recipe, or for a long time, as in a stew or sauce.

Squid Stew with Tomatoes and Olives

In Naples, this is called pignatello Frisio, *after a famous restaurant of the same name, which used to be a meeting place for writers and artists at the beginning of the century. Try to make this long-simmered, sunny Neapolitan stew with ripe summer tomatoes. Serve with steamed rice.*

Makes 6 servings

3 tablespoons extra-virgin olive oil
3 pounds squid, tentacles cut off and reserved, squid cut into ½-inch-wide rings
1 pound ripe plum tomatoes, peeled, seeded, and cut into ½-inch-wide strips
1 tablespoon capers, drained
¾ cup black Mediterranean olives, pitted
⅛ teaspoon crushed hot pepper flakes
Salt
1 tablespoon chopped fresh parsley

1) In a large Dutch oven, heat the olive oil over medium heat. Add all the squid and cook, stirring often, until the squid is opaque and gives off its juices, about 5 minutes. Cover and reduce the heat to low. Simmer until the squid is tender, about 45 minutes.

2) Add the tomatoes, capers, olives, and hot pepper. Cover and simmer until the tomatoes have formed a sauce, about 15 minutes. Season with salt to taste. Sprinkle with the parsley and serve from the pot in deep soup bowls.

Pasta and Risotto

In Italy, pasta and rice (usually in the form of a risotto) are not commonly served as side dishes. Both are eaten all by themselves, usually as a first course before the fish or meat. Here in America, we've taken things a step farther and elevated pasta, the most popular of foods—or rice—to a main course.

This transition works delightfully well for the one-pot classics in this chapter, though, if you prefer, of course you could serve any one as a starter. I've included a selection of both lightly sauced pastas, such as Pasta all'Arrabbiata and Cavatelli with Arugula and Tomato Sauce, and more richly coated pastas, such as Spaghetti with Three Cheeses and Potato Gnocchi Flor-

entine (which always signifies spinach). Almost all
these recipes are simple, but it is most important that
the pasta be properly cooked.

Always cook your pasta in plenty of water in a large
pasta pot, not in a huge stockpot, which is too heavy
and will require too long for the water to return to the
boil after you add the pasta. The water for the pot
should be heavily salted, and the salt should be added
after the water boils. I add 2 tablespoons of coarse ko-
sher salt to every 4 quarts of water. Pasta is bland, and
if it is well seasoned as it cooks, the sauce will need
much less salt. *Never* add oil to the water. It will make
the sauce slide off the pasta, and you want the sauce to
adhere. After the salted water comes to a boil, add the
pasta and stir with a long fork or pasta spoon. Cover
the pot and let the water return to a boil. Then uncover or set the cover askew and cook the pasta at a
constant boil according to the time given in the recipe
or in the instructions on your pasta package. Taste
often during the last few minutes. You want the pasta
tender but with a little resistance in the middle: al
dente. For many dishes, I suggest reserving a cup of
the cooking water to add to the pastas if necessary. To
stop the cooking immediately, add a cup of cold water.
Drain the pasta into a colander and turn into a pasta

bowl, which should be shallow and not too deep; then toss with the sauce. Do not overdrain the pasta. The Neapolitans, residents of Naples, who are masters of cooking spaghetti say *"lo spaghetto con la goccia,"* literally "the spaghetti with a drop," meaning a little wet.

Americans have only recently fallen in love with risotto, but it is a love affair that is destined to grow, especially as more and more cooks master the simple art of cooking this rice properly. Risottos make perfect one-pot dinners. With my instructions, I think you will produce perfect risotto every time. Just remember to use real Arborio or other Italian short-grain rice to produce the creaminess of a well-made risotto and still retain the al dente center of the rice.

In the few rice casseroles at the end of this chapter, you may be surprised to see me call for converted rice and even instant rice. Well, that is because these products produce the easiest and the best results in these recipes, and I believe food can be both classic and modern at the same time. After you taste them, I hope you agree.

Pasta all'Arrabbiata

This variant on "angry" pasta
is so named because the hot chile pepper attacks your palate.
But with today's fondness for spicy foods, it will seem tamer than
it did to yesterday's eaters. Like the original, the sauce is quick
and easy to make.

Makes 4 to 6 servings

2 medium carrots, peeled and cut
  crosswise in half
2 tablespoons extra-virgin olive
  oil
2 scallions (white parts and
  1 inch of green tops),
  chopped
1 (2-ounce) can flat anchovy
  fillets, drained and coarsely
  chopped

1 dried hot red pepper or ¼ to
  ½ teaspoon crushed hot
  pepper flakes, to taste
1 cup canned crushed tomatoes
¾ cup black Mediterranean
  olives, pitted and coarsely
  chopped
Salt
1 pound penne
1 tablespoon chopped parsley

1) In a large pot of boiling salted water, cook the carrots until barely
tender, 5 to 7 minutes. Drain and rinse under cold water. When cool
enough to handle, cut the carrots into thin rounds and set aside.

2) In the same pot, heat the olive oil over medium heat. Add the carrots,
scallions, anchovies, and hot pepper. Cook, stirring, until the scallions
are softened, about 1 minute. Stir in the tomatoes and ½ cup water. Bring to
a simmer. Reduce the heat to medium-low and cook, stirring often, until
slightly thickened, about 15 minutes. Stir in the olives. Transfer to a heated
bowl and set aside. Rinse out the pot.

3) In the same pot, bring 4 quarts of water to a rapid boil. Salt
generously, add the penne, and cook until tender but still firm, 10 to 12
minutes. Drain in a colander.

4) Return the sauce to the pasta pot and reheat for a minute or two. Add
the penne and cook, stirring gently, until heated through, about 1 minute.
Transfer to a pasta serving bowl, sprinkle with the parsley, and serve immediately.

Cavatelli with Arugula and Tomato Sauce

*T*he slightly spicy taste of *arugula adds zest to this specialty of Apulia, a region in southern Italy. Cavatelli are semolina and flour dumplings, with a shell shape that catches every last drop of sauce. Don't overboil them; they will also simmer in the sauce. Cavatelli can be found in the frozen food department of Italian grocery stores and many supermarkets.*

Makes 4 to 6 servings

3 bunches of arugula, rinsed, tough stems trimmed, leaves cut into 2-inch pieces (about 3 packed cups)
1 pound frozen cavatelli
3 tablespoons extra-virgin olive oil

2 garlic cloves, minced
1 (16-ounce) can peeled plum tomatoes, coarsely chopped, juices reserved
⅛ teaspoon freshly ground pepper
Grated Romano cheese

1) In a large pot of boiling salted water, cook the arugula and cavatelli until the pasta is just tender but still firm, 8 to 10 minutes. Drain in a colander. Transfer to a bowl, toss with 1 tablespoon of the olive oil, cover, and set aside.

2) In the same pot, heat the remaining oil and the garlic over medium heat. When the garlic is sizzling, add the tomatoes with their juices and the pepper. Cook, stirring often, until the sauce is slightly thickened, about 15 minutes.

3) Add the cavatelli and arugula to the sauce in the pot. Reduce the heat to medium-low. Cook, stirring often, until the cavatelli are tender, about 5 minutes. Serve immediately in a warm bowl. Pass a bowl of Romano cheese on the side.

Rotelle with Garlicky Broccoli Sauce

Fast and savory, this pasta dish is pleasingly scented with fresh garlic and fine olive oil. The sauce would be equally good with bow-tie pasta.

Makes 4 to 6 servings

Salt
1 pound rotelle or bow-tie pasta
1 medium bunch of broccoli, trimmed and cut into florets (about 3 cups)
2 medium carrots, finely diced
¼ cup extra-virgin olive oil

5 garlic cloves, minced
2 ripe plum tomatoes, seeded and chopped
3 tablespoons chopped fresh basil
⅛ teaspoon freshly ground pepper

1) Bring a large pot of water to a boil over high heat. Salt generously and add the pasta, broccoli, and carrots. Cook until the pasta is tender but firm and the vegetables well cooked, about 10 minutes. Scoop out 1 cup of the cooking liquid and set aside. Drain the pasta and vegetables in a colander. Dry the pot.

2) In the same pot, heat the olive oil and garlic over medium heat. When the garlic is sizzling, add the tomatoes, basil, ¼ teaspoon salt, and the pepper. Cook just until the tomatoes release their juices, about 3 minutes. Return the pasta and vegetables to the pot. Cook, tossing, just until heated through, about 1 minute. If the dish seems dry, add a little of the reserved pasta cooking liquid. Serve hot or at room temperature.

Spaghetti with Three Cheeses

For a late-night supper with friends, after the theater or a night on the town, I often toss together this luxuriously rich pasta. (In Italy, this kind of impromptu pasta meal is called a spaghettata.) You must use Italian fontina d'Aosta cheese, not the Swedish imitation. Mascarpone is a buttery, spreadable cheese that we know chiefly as the main ingredient for tiramisù. Both cheeses can be found at Italian grocers, specialty cheese stores, and many supermarkets. **Makes 4 to 6 servings**

4 ounces mascarpone or cream cheese, at room temperature
⅓ cup heavy cream
3 tablespoons grated Parmesan cheese, plus additional for serving
¼ teaspoon grated nutmeg
¼ teaspoon freshly ground pepper
1 pound spaghetti
4 ounces Italian fontina cheese, cut into thin strips

1) In a large pasta bowl, mix together the mascarpone cheese, heavy cream, 3 tablespoons of the Parmesan cheese, nutmeg, and pepper until smooth. Set aside at room temperature.

2) In a large pot of boiling salted water, cook the spaghetti until tender but still firm, 10 to 12 minutes. Scoop out 1 cup of the cooking water and set aside. Drain the spaghetti into a colander, but do not shake dry.

3) Pour the hot pasta over the mascarpone mixture and quickly toss, adding as much of the reserved cooking water as needed to make a smooth sauce. Add the fontina cheese and toss again lightly. Serve immediately in warm bowls. Pass a bowl of grated Parmesan cheese.

Fettuccine with Swiss Chard and Ham

Swiss chard could stand to be
known a little better by American cooks. European cooks love
it—it is a little sturdier than spinach, its close cousin, and the stalks
can be eaten, too. Stirred into tomato sauce with a little ham,
it makes a fine pasta sauce. **Makes 4 to 6 servings**

1 pound Swiss chard, well
  washed
1 pound dried fettuccine
3 cups Basic Tomato Sauce
  (recipe follows)

¼ pound thickly sliced smoked
  ham, cut into thin strips
Freshly ground pepper
Grated Parmesan cheese

1) Cut the thick stalks off the Swiss chard and cut crosswise into ¼-inch-thick pieces. A few at a time, stack the leaves and cut into large pieces about 3 inches square.

2) In a large pasta pot, bring 4 quarts of lightly salted water to a boil over high heat. Add the pasta and chard stalks and cook for 5 minutes. Add the chard leaves and cook until the pasta is tender but still firm, 3 to 5 minutes longer. Drain the pasta and chard in a colander.

3) Add the tomato sauce and the ham to the pot and cook over medium heat until hot. Return the pasta to the pot, add the remaining sauce, and toss over heat for a few more minutes. Season with pepper to taste. Serve in warm bowls. Pass a bowl of Parmesan cheese on the side.

Basic Tomato Sauce

This simple and flavorful
*tomato sauce is called "fake" (*sugo finto*), because the
combination of vegetables makes it taste as if it has meat in it. Of
course, you can't accuse it of being an impostor if you use the
optional prosciutto. Don't puree fresh tomatoes in a food
processor—the blades chop the seeds and make them bitter.*

Makes about 3 cups

3 tablespoons extra-virgin olive
  oil
¼ pound prosciutto, finely
  chopped (optional)
1 medium onion, chopped
1 medium carrot, chopped
1 medium celery rib, chopped
1 teaspoon chopped fresh sage
  or ¼ teaspoon dried
1 teaspoon chopped parsley

1 teaspoon tomato paste
3 pounds ripe plum tomatoes,
  peeled and seeded, or
  3 (15-ounce) cans peeled
  tomatoes, drained
1 tablespoon chopped fresh basil
  or ½ teaspoon dried
1 tablespoon butter
Salt
Freshly ground pepper

1) In a large pot, heat 2 tablespoons of the olive oil over medium heat.
Add the prosciutto, if using, the onion, carrot, celery, sage, and parsley.
Cook, stirring often, until the vegetables soften, 5 to 8 minutes. Add the
tomato paste and stir for 1 minute.

2) Meanwhile, puree the tomatoes in a food mill or by rubbing through
a coarse wire sieve. Add to the pot and bring to a simmer. Stir in the basil
and reduce the heat to medium-low. Simmer, stirring often, until the sauce
thickens, about 30 minutes. Remove from the heat and stir in the
remaining 1 tablespoon oil (or use the butter instead). Season with salt and
pepper to taste.

Smoky Pasta with Green Sauce

Smoked mozzarella isn't found in too many pasta recipes, and it's a pleasant surprise in this easy-to-make dish. Look for it at Italian grocers' and in many supermarkets. **Makes 4 to 6 servings**

2 cups ricotta, well drained
1 (10-ounce) package frozen chopped spinach, cooked and squeezed to remove moisture
2 ounces Genoa salami, finely chopped
2 tablespoons grated Parmesan cheese

½ teaspoon freshly ground pepper
1 pound penne, fusilli, or rigatoni
¾ pound smoked mozzarella cheese or smoked Edam cheese, diced
½ pound fresh mozzarella cheese, diced

1) In a pasta serving bowl, combine the drained ricotta, spinach, salami, Parmesan cheese, and pepper. Set aside at room temperature.

2) In a large pot of boiling salted water, cook the penne until tender but still firm, 10 to 12 minutes. Scoop out 1 cup of the cooking water and set aside. Drain the penne in a colander.

3) Add the hot pasta to the ricotta mixture and toss, adding as much of the reserved cooking water as needed to make a smooth sauce. Scatter the smoked and fresh mozzarella cheeses on top and toss again. Serve immediately in warm bowls.

Penne with Fresh Tomatoes, Mozzarella, and Basil

F*ragrantly fresh and simple to make, this recipe must be prepared only in summer, when tomatoes are at their best. This is one of the few pasta recipes that can be enjoyed at room temperature because we Italians don't particularly like cold pasta. Italian* mozzarella di bufala, *made from water buffalo milk, is the best. It can be found in many Italian grocery shops or specialty cheese stores, but use regular fresh or packaged mozzarella if buffalo mozzarella is unavailable.*

Makes 4 to 6 servings

5 ripe medium tomatoes (about
  1½ pounds), seeded and
  coarsely chopped
¼ cup extra-virgin olive oil
⅓ cup chopped fresh basil
1 tablespoon chopped parsley
1 garlic clove, minced

¼ teaspoon freshly ground
  pepper
1 pound penne or rigatoni
½ pound fresh mozzarella
  cheese, preferably bufala, cut
  into ½-inch dice
Salt

1) About 1 hour before serving, in a pasta serving bowl, combine the tomatoes, olive oil, basil, parsley, garlic, and pepper. Cover and let the fresh tomato sauce stand at cool room temperature until ready to serve.

2) In a large pot of boiling salted water, cook the penne until tender but still firm, 10 to 12 minutes. Drain in a colander.

3) Add the hot pasta to the sauce in the bowl and toss gently. Add the mozzarella, season with salt to taste, toss again, and serve.

Pasta Shells with Pumpkin Sauce

This is a great dish for an autumn dinner. America has such wonderful pumpkins, but they should be used for more than pie! Small pumpkins, which are often found at farmers' markets or produce stands, are excellent for cooking. Otherwise, choose the smallest jack o'lantern pumpkin available—they are drier and less stringy than the large ones. Other winter squashes, such as Hubbard, butternut, or acorn, can also be used. ***Makes 4 to 6 servings***

1 small pumpkin (2 pounds), stem cut off
3 tablespoons extra-virgin olive oil
1 large onion, sliced
1 garlic clove, minced
2 small green bell peppers, seeded and chopped

2 cups canned tomato puree
3 tablespoons chopped fresh basil
¼ teaspoon salt
⅛ teaspoon freshly ground pepper
1 pound medium pasta shells

1) Preheat the oven to 350 degrees F. Cut the pumpkin in half vertically. Scoop out and discard the seeds and filaments. Place the pumpkin halves, cut side up, in a shallow baking dish and add 1 cup water to the dish. Bake until the pumpkin is slightly softened, about 20 minutes. Cut into slices, peel the slices, then cut into 1-inch cubes.

2) In a large pot, heat the olive oil over medium heat. Add the onion and garlic and cook, stirring often, until the onion is softened and translucent, 3 to 5 minutes. Add the bell peppers and cook until softened, about 5 minutes. Add the pumpkin cubes and cook, stirring often, for 5 minutes. Add the tomato puree, 1 cup water, the basil, salt, and pepper. Bring to a simmer. Reduce the heat to medium-low and cover. Cook until the pumpkin is tender, about 15 minutes. Transfer the pumpkin sauce to a serving bowl. Rinse out the pot.

3) In the same pot, bring 4 quarts of water to a rapid boil. Salt generously and add the pasta. Cook until just tender, 10 to 12 minutes. Scoop out 1 cup of the pasta cooking liquid and set aside. Drain the pasta in a colander.

4) Return the pasta to the pot. Add the pumpkin sauce and cook over medium heat, tossing gently to heat through, 2 to 3 minutes, adding some of the reserved cooking liquid if necessary. Place in the serving bowl and serve immediately.

Artichoke and Prosciutto Timballo

Makes 4 to 6 servings

2 tablespoons butter, cut into
small pieces
4 tablespoons dried unflavored
bread crumbs
4 cups cooked tubular pasta,
such as rigatoni, penne, or
ziti
3 cups Basic Tomato Sauce
(page 117)
1 (10-ounce) package frozen
artichoke hearts, thawed and
coarsely chopped

¼ cup plus 3 tablespoons grated
Parmesan cheese
2 eggs, beaten
¼ teaspoon freshly ground
pepper
1 pound mozzarella cheese,
thinly sliced
¼ pound sliced prosciutto, cut
into thin strips
2 hard-cooked eggs, cut into
thin rounds

1) Preheat the oven to 375 degrees F. Use half the butter to generously coat the inside of a 10-inch springform pan. Coat the inside of the pan with 2 tablespoons of the bread crumbs, tapping out the excess crumbs.

2) In a large bowl, stir together the cooked pasta, half of the tomato sauce, the artichoke hearts, 3 tablespoons of the Parmesan cheese, the beaten eggs, and the pepper. Pour one-third of the pasta mixture into the pan. Top with one half of the sliced mozzarella, the prosciutto, and hard-cooked eggs. Spoon on some of the remaining tomato sauce. Sprinkle with 2 tablespoons of the Parmesan cheese. Add half of the remaining pasta mixture and top with the remaining sliced mozzarella, prosciutto, and eggs. Cover with the remaining sauce. Sprinkle the remaining 2 tablespoons each Parmesan cheese and bread crumbs over the top, then dot with the remaining butter.

3) Bake until golden brown, about 40 minutes. Let stand for 10 minutes. Invert the timballo onto a serving plate. Cut into wedges to serve.

Timballo of Penne and Cheese

A timballo can often be quite elaborate and is served unmolded. It is a genuine Italian classic. This homey version uses leftover penne layered with ripe fresh tomatoes (a must), basil, and mozzarella cheese, and is no less excellent just because it's uncomplicated.

Makes 4 to 6 servings

5½ tablespoons extra-virgin olive oil
½ cup plain dried bread crumbs
4 cups cooked penne
1 cup chopped fresh basil
¼ cup grated Romano cheese
2 eggs, beaten
¼ teaspoon salt

⅛ teaspoon freshly ground pepper
8 medium tomatoes (about 2 pounds), peeled, seeded, and cut into ½-inch-thick slices
1 pound whole milk mozzarella cheese, thinly sliced

1) Preheat the oven to 375 degrees F. With 1½ teaspoons oil, lightly coat a 2½-quart round baking dish. Dust with 2 tablespoons of the bread crumbs; tap out any excess.

2) In a large bowl, toss the penne with the basil, 1 tablespoon of the bread crumbs, 2 tablespoons of the olive oil, 1 tablespoon of the Romano cheese, the eggs, salt, and pepper.

3) Place one-third of the pasta in a prepared baking dish. Cover with half of the tomatoes and mozzarella, then sprinkle on 1½ tablespoons Romano cheese and drizzle on 1 tablespoon oil. Add half of the remaining pasta and cover with the remaining tomatoes, mozzarella, Romano, and 1 tablespoon oil. Top with the remaining pasta. Sprinkle with the remaining bread crumbs and drizzle with the remaining 1 tablespoon oil.

4) Bake until the top is golden brown, 35 to 45 minutes. Let stand 10 minutes before serving.

Potato Gnocchi Florentine

Another easy dish that comes together with no trouble at all. Classic gnocchi are made with potatoes, which gives them a nice resilient texture. They can be found in the frozen food department of the supermarket and at Italian grocery stores.

Makes 4 to 6 servings

1½ pounds frozen potato gnocchi
1½ pounds fresh spinach, thick stems removed, leaves cut into 2-inch-wide strips
6 tablespoons butter, at room temperature

½ cup heavy cream
1 tablespoon tomato paste
¼ teaspoon salt
⅛ teaspoon freshly ground pepper
1 cup shredded Parmesan cheese

1) In a large pot of boiling salted water, cook the gnocchi until they are tender and float on the surface of the water, about 5 minutes. Stir in the spinach and return to a boil, about 1 minute. Scoop out about 1 cup of the cooking water and set aside. Drain the gnocchi and spinach in a colander. Place in a large serving bowl. Add 2 tablespoons of the butter and toss well. Cover to keep warm.

2) In the same pot, bring the remaining 4 tablespoons butter, the cream, tomato paste, salt, and pepper to a simmer over medium-low heat, stirring to dissolve the tomato paste. Return the gnocchi and spinach to the pot. Toss to coat with sauce and reheat, adding enough of the reserved cooking water, if needed, to make a sauce that nicely coats the pasta. Add the Parmesan cheese and toss again. Return to the serving bowl and serve immediately.

Fusilli with Tuna Puttanesca Sauce

We Italians have an ingenious knack for combining flavorful ingredients in simple ways to make wonderful food, like this family version of the classic quick tuna sauce from Naples.

Makes 4 to 6 servings

1 (6-ounce) can Italian tuna packed in olive oil, oil reserved
4 ripe medium tomatoes, peeled, seeded, and coarsely chopped
1 small red onion, thinly sliced
⅓ cup pitted black olives, coarsely chopped

1½ tablespoons capers, rinsed and drained
⅓ cup chopped fresh basil
1 tablespoon chopped parsley
1 garlic clove, crushed through a press
⅛ teaspoon freshly ground pepper
1 pound fusilli

1) In a large serving bowl, combine all of the ingredients except the pasta. Mix well, coarsely breaking up the tuna; it should retain some texture. Cover and set aside for up to 1 hour.

2) In a large pot of boiling salted water, cook the fusilli until tender but still firm, 10 to 12 minutes. Drain in a colander.

3) Add the pasta to the sauce and toss well. Serve immediately.

Tortellini with Goose Liver Pâté

This scrumptious pasta should be made with the best goose liver pâté you can afford. It's quite rich, and some cooks may prefer to serve it in small portions as a first course. ***Makes 4 to 6 servings***

1 pound fresh or frozen meat- or
   cheese-filled tortellini
1 cup heavy cream
2 tablespoons dry Marsala wine
¼ teaspoon salt
⅛ teaspoon freshly ground
   pepper

6 ounces goose liver pâté, cut
   into ½-inch cubes
2 cups shredded mozzarella
   cheese (½ pound)
Grated Parmesan cheese

1) In a large pot, bring 4 quarts of salted water to a rapid boil. Add the tortellini and cook until tender, about 3 minutes (6 minutes for frozen tortellini). Scoop out about 1 cup of the cooking water and set aside. Drain the tortellini in a colander.

2) Pour the cream and Marsala into the pasta pot and bring to a boil, 1 to 2 minutes. Season with the salt and pepper.

3) Transfer the tortellini to a large serving bowl. Pour on the hot Marsala cream and toss. Add the goose liver pâté and mozzarella. Mix gently, adding some of the reserved cooking water, if necessary, to make a smoother sauce that nicely coats the pasta. Serve immediately in warmed bowls. Pass a bowl of Parmesan cheese at the table.

Bow-Ties with Shrimp and Peas

I *usually serve this colorful pasta as soon as it is done. During hot weather, you can let it cool to room temperature, but* never *serve it chilled. (You have to look long and hard to find an Italian cook who endorses pasta salads!)*

Makes 4 to 6 servings

1 pound medium shrimp, peeled and deveined, shells reserved
2 sprigs of parsley
1 bay leaf
1 pound bow-tie pasta
1 cup peas, fresh or frozen
½ pound thickly sliced prosciutto, cut into ½-inch dice
½ pound mozzarella cheese, preferably fresh, cut into ½-inch dice

3 ripe medium tomatoes, peeled, seeded, and chopped
¼ cup chopped fresh basil
3 tablespoons extra-virgin olive oil
1 garlic clove, minced
2 hard-cooked eggs, sliced into rounds

1) Wrap the shrimp shells, parsley, and bay leaf in a piece of cheesecloth. Place in a large pot and add 4 quarts lightly salted water. Bring to a rapid boil over high heat. Reduce the heat to low and simmer for 15 minutes. Discard the cheesecloth bundle. Add the shrimp and cook until firm and bright pink, 3 to 5 minutes. Using a skimmer or a slotted spoon, transfer the shrimp to a bowl and set aside.

2) Return the water to a rapid boil. Add the bow-tie pasta and cook until tender but still firm, about 10 minutes. During the last 2 minutes, add the peas (5 minutes if using fresh peas). Drain the pasta in a colander.

3) Return the pasta to the pot. Add the reserved shrimp, the prosciutto, mozzarella, tomatoes, basil, olive oil, and garlic; toss.

4) Transfer to a warm serving bowl. Garnish with the sliced eggs and serve immediately.

Linguine and Seafood
al Cartoccio

Here's pasta with a twist, a specialty of restaurants on the Adriatic coast where it is served with appropriate flair. The ingredients are wrapped in a foil "pouch" (cartoccio) and baked. When you open the parcel at the table, you experience a subtle marine essence and the pungent perfume of garlic and basil. For best results, use extra-width, heavy-duty aluminum foil.   **Makes 6 servings**

1 pound mussels, scrubbed and beards removed
12 littleneck clams, scrubbed
1 tablespoon flour
¾ pound linguine
¼ cup extra-virgin olive oil
3 garlic cloves, crushed through a press
⅛ teaspoon crushed hot red pepper flakes

1½ pounds monkfish, cut into 1-inch cubes
1 pound medium shrimp, peeled and deveined
2 pints cherry tomatoes, each cut lengthwise in half
⅓ cup chopped fresh basil

1) In a large bowl, sprinkle the mussels and clams with the flour. Add enough cold water to cover. Let stand for 30 to 60 minutes. Drain and rinse well. (This step helps remove any grit from the shellfish.)

2) Meanwhile, in a large pot of boiling salted water, cook the linguine until just tender, 10 to 12 minutes. Drain in a colander. Toss with 1 tablespoon of the olive oil and set aside.

3) Put the mussels and clams into the pasta pot. Cover and cook over medium heat, shaking the pot often, until the shellfish are all opened, about 5 minutes. Using a slotted spoon, remove the shellfish. Reserve the shellfish meat; discard the shells and any mussels or clams that do not open. Strain the shellfish liquid into a medium bowl through a fine sieve lined with a paper towel. Reserve the shellfish liquid. Rinse out the pot and wipe dry. Preheat the oven to 375 degrees F.

4) In the same pot, heat the remaining 3 tablespoons oil over medium heat. Add the garlic and hot pepper and cook until the garlic is fragrant, about 1 minute. Add the monkfish and the shellfish cooking liquid. Cook for 3 minutes. Add the shrimp and cherry tomatoes and cook until the shrimp start to turn pink, 2 to 3 minutes. Stir in the reserved shellfish and linguine and the basil. Toss to mix well.

5) Place 6 squares of heavy-duty aluminum foil on a flat work surface. Divide the pasta mixture among the foil squares. Bring up the 4 corners and twist to seal. Set the foil pouches on a large baking sheet. Bake 15 to 20 minutes. Slide the foil pouches onto individual plates and let your guests open them.

Penne with Seafood Oreganata

In the charming Neapolitan district of Marechiaro, cooks rushing to make dinner in a hurry combine their glorious local seafood and tomatoes to create this wonderful pasta dish. If you wish, substitute 2½ pounds ripe plum tomatoes, peeled, seeded, and pureed, for the canned tomatoes.

Makes 4 to 6 servings

1 pound dried penne
3 tablespoons extra-virgin olive oil
2 garlic cloves, finely chopped
1 (28-ounce) can crushed tomatoes
2 tablespoons chopped parsley
½ teaspoon dried oregano

⅛ to ¼ teaspoon crushed hot red pepper
1 pound flounder fillets
18 littleneck clams or mussels, scrubbed, mussel beards removed
Freshly ground pepper

1) In a large pot of boiling salted water, cook the pasta until tender but still firm, 9 to 12 minutes. Scoop out and reserve 1 cup of the cooking water. Drain the penne in a colander and toss with 1 tablespoon of the olive oil.

2) In the same pot, heat the remaining 2 tablespoons oil over medium heat. Add the garlic and cook until golden, about 1 minute. Stir in the reserved cooking water, crushed tomatoes, 1 tablespoon of the parsley, the oregano, and the hot pepper. Bring to a simmer. Reduce the heat to medium-low and simmer until slightly thickened, 10 to 15 minutes.

3) Add the flounder and cook for 3 minutes. Add the clams or mussels and increase the heat to medium. Cover and cook until the clams or mussels open, about 5 minutes. Using a slotted spoon, transfer the shellfish to a bowl. Cover to keep warm.

4) Return the pasta to the pot. Stir, breaking up the flounder with a spoon. Season with pepper to taste. Serve in warm bowls, topping each serving with a few clams or mussels in their shells and a sprinkling of the remaining parsley.

Spaghetti Frittata with Portobello Mushrooms

Plan ahead, and next time you
have spaghetti for dinner, make extra to provide the leftovers
needed to make this Italian classic. **Makes 3 to 4 servings**

3 tablespoons extra-virgin olive
  oil
1 garlic clove, minced
2 portobello mushrooms, cut
  into ½-inch slices (cut
  mushrooms in half before
  slicing if they are very large)
¼ teaspoon salt
¼ teaspoon freshly ground
  pepper

2 tablespoons chopped parsley
3 eggs
3 tablespoons grated Parmesan
  cheese
2 cups cooked spaghetti, cut into
  2-inch lengths
⅛ teaspoon freshly ground
  pepper

1) Preheat the oven to 375 degrees F. In a medium cast-iron skillet, heat
1 tablespoon of the olive oil over medium heat. Add the garlic and cook
until fragrant, about 1 minute. Add the mushrooms, salt, and ⅛ teaspoon of
the pepper. Cook, stirring occasionally, until the mushrooms begin to
brown, 8 to 10 minutes. Stir in 1 tablespoon of the parsley. Transfer to a plate.
Wipe out the skillet with paper towels.

2) In a medium bowl, beat the eggs, Parmesan cheese, and the
remaining parsley and pepper. Stir in the spaghetti and mushrooms.

3) In the same skillet, heat the remaining oil over medium heat. Pour in
the egg mixture. As the edges set, lift them up with a spatula and tilt the
pan so the uncooked eggs flow underneath. Continue cooking until the
frittata is set but the top is still shiny, about 3 minutes.

4) Transfer to the oven and bake 10 minutes, or until the top is golden.
Transfer the frittata to a warmed round platter and serve immediately.

Risotto with Cabbage, Pink Beans, and Red Wine

In Novara, in the Piedmont region, this is called paniscia. *It is just the kind of warming fare to serve on a cold winter night.* **Makes 4 to 6 servings**

4 tablespoons butter
2 tablespoons finely chopped prosciutto fat or butter
¼ pound Genoa salami, chopped
1 medium onion, chopped
1 medium carrot, cut into ¼-inch dice
1 medium celery rib, cut into ¼-inch dice
4 cups shredded green cabbage, preferably Savoy cabbage

1½ cups Arborio rice
½ cup dry red wine
2 bay leaves
6 to 7 cups chicken broth or hot water
1 (19-ounce) can Roman or pink beans, drained and rinsed
Salt and freshly ground pepper
Grated Parmesan cheese

1) In a large Dutch oven, heat 2 tablespoons of the butter and the prosciutto fat over medium heat. Add the salami, onion, carrot, and celery. Cook, stirring often, until the vegetables soften, about 5 minutes. Add the cabbage and cover. Cook until the cabbage wilts, about 5 minutes.

2) Add the rice and cook, uncovered, stirring often, until the rice is well coated, 2 to 3 minutes. Stir in the wine and bay leaves. Cook until the wine reduces by half, about 3 minutes. Add 1 cup broth and reduce the heat to medium. Cook, stirring constantly, until the rice almost completely absorbs the liquid, about 3 minutes. Continue adding broth 1 cup at a time, stirring constantly, waiting until it is almost completely absorbed before adding more. When the last cup of broth is added, stir in the beans. Remove and discard the bay leaves, stir in the remaining butter, and season with salt and pepper to taste. Serve immediately in warmed bowls. Pass grated Parmesan cheese on the side.

Risotto with Green Beans and Italian Sausage

I *think of this risotto as a song that can be played in many variations. Sometimes I'll substitute broccoli, peas, or artichoke hearts for the green beans. For a heartier dish, I'll stir in some cooked white beans. It's always delicious.*

Makes 4 to 6 servings

5 cups water
2 cups chicken broth, homemade or low-sodium canned
½ pound green beans, trimmed and cut into ½-inch pieces
1 tablespoon extra-virgin olive oil
¾ pound sweet Italian sausage, cut into 1-inch pieces

1 medium red onion, chopped
1½ cups Arborio rice
¼ teaspoon salt
¼ teaspoon freshly ground pepper
1 tablespoon butter
Grated Parmesan cheese

1) In a large Dutch oven, bring the water and broth to a boil over high heat. Add the green beans and cook until tender, 4 to 5 minutes. Strain the green beans through a colander set over a large bowl. Reserve the broth and keep hot. Set the beans aside.

2) In the same Dutch oven, heat the oil over medium heat. Add the sausage and cook, stirring often, until lightly browned, about 6 minutes. Add the onion and cook, stirring often, until it softens, about 5 minutes.

3) Add the rice. Cook, stirring constantly, 2 to 3 minutes. Add 1 cup of the reserved broth and reduce the heat to medium. Cook, stirring constantly, until the rice almost completely absorbs the broth, about 3 minutes. Continue adding the broth 1 cup at a time, stirring constantly, waiting until it is almost completely absorbed before adding more. When the last cup of broth is added, stir in the green beans, salt, and pepper. Just before serving, stir in the butter. Serve immediately in warmed bowls. Pass grated Parmesan cheese on the side.

Risotto with Meat and Peas

My dear friend Enzo Lunardi *gave me this recipe of his mother's. It gets extra flavor from chopped chicken livers and ground meat. Italians would certainly use ground veal, but ground turkey, an excellent substitute, is easier to find here, and usually less expensive.* **Makes 6 servings**

2 tablespoons butter
1 tablespoon extra-virgin olive
  oil
2 medium leeks (white and
  tender green), finely chopped
  and rinsed well
1 medium celery rib, finely
  chopped
½ pound ground veal or turkey

3 chicken livers, trimmed and cut
  into ½-inch cubes
½ teaspoon salt
⅛ teaspoon freshly ground
  pepper
2 cups Arborio rice
6 to 7 cups hot chicken broth
1½ cups fresh or frozen peas
Grated Parmesan cheese

1) In a large heavy saucepan or Dutch oven, melt the butter in the oil over medium-high heat. Add the leeks and celery. Cook, stirring often, until softened, 3 to 5 minutes.

2) Add the ground veal and cook, stirring occasionally, until the meat loses its pink color, 4 to 6 minutes. Add the livers, salt, and pepper. Cook, stirring often, until the livers are lightly browned, about 5 minutes.

3) Add the rice and stir for 1 minute. Add 1 cup of the broth and reduce the heat to medium. Cook, stirring constantly, until the rice absorbs the broth, about 3 minutes. Continue adding the broth 1 cup at a time, stirring constantly, waiting until it is almost completely absorbed before adding more. Stir in the peas. At the end, the rice should be tender and slightly creamy. Serve immediately. Pass a bowl of grated Parmesan cheese.

Chicken and Vegetable Risotto

Makes 4 servings

2 tablespoons extra-virgin olive oil, plus more as needed
1 garlic clove, crushed under a knife
1 small red bell pepper, seeded and cut into ½-inch squares
½ teaspoon dried rosemary
1 medium onion, chopped
1 medium carrot, chopped
½ cup canned crushed tomatoes

1½ cups Arborio rice
About 6 cups hot chicken broth
½ cup thawed frozen peas
¼ teaspoon salt
⅛ teaspoon freshly ground pepper
2 cups leftover cooked chicken, cut into 1-inch pieces
2 tablespoons grated Parmesan cheese, plus more for serving

1) In a heavy-bottomed Dutch oven, heat the olive oil over medium heat. Add the garlic and cook until fragrant, about 1 minute. Add the bell pepper and cook, stirring often, until tender, about 10 minutes. Using a slotted spoon, transfer the pepper to a bowl, discarding the garlic.

2) If necessary, add a little more oil to the Dutch oven. Add the rosemary, onion, and carrot. Cook over medium heat, stirring often, until the vegetables soften, about 5 minutes. Add the tomatoes, reduce the heat to medium-low and simmer until slightly thickened, about 10 minutes.

3) Add the rice. Cook, stirring constantly, until it absorbs the cooking liquid, about 3 minutes. Add 1 cup of the broth and reduce the heat to medium-low. Simmer, stirring constantly, until the rice almost completely absorbs the broth, about 3 minutes. Continue adding the broth 1 cup at a time, stirring constantly, waiting until it is almost completely absorbed before adding more. When 1 cup of the broth remains, stir in the bell pepper, peas, salt, and pepper. Place the chicken in the center of the rice. Pour the remaining broth over all and cover. Reduce the heat to very low and cook until the rice is tender and slightly creamy and the chicken is hot, about 5 minutes. Sprinkle with 2 tablespoons of the cheese. Serve immediately in warmed bowls, with a bowl of Parmesan cheese on the side.

Risotto with Chicken Livers and Mushrooms

*C*hicken livers, mushrooms, and marsala wine are a well-loved trio in the Italian kitchen. Marsala wine comes in two varieties, dry and sweet, so read the label carefully. Dry Marsala should be used in savory cooking, as here, and the sweet in desserts. **Makes 4 to 6 servings**

¼ cup dried porcini mushrooms
3 tablespoons extra-virgin olive oil
1 pound chicken livers, trimmed, each cut in half
½ teaspoon salt
¼ teaspoon freshly ground pepper
½ cup dry Marsala wine

1 medium onion, chopped
4 ounces fresh white button mushrooms, quartered
1½ cups Arborio rice
6 cups hot chicken broth
1 tablespoon butter
1 tablespoon chopped parsley
Grated Parmesan cheese

1) In a small bowl, cover the dried porcini with 1 cup lukewarm water and let stand until softened, about 15 minutes. Lift out the mushrooms and chop coarsely. Strain the soaking liquid through a sieve lined with a moistened paper towel; reserve the liquid.

2) In a large skillet, heat 2 tablespoons olive oil over medium-high heat. Add the livers, ¼ teaspoon salt, and ⅛ teaspoon pepper. Cook, turning occasionally, until the livers are browned, about 6 minutes. Add 2 tablespoons of the Marsala and cook until it evaporates, 1 to 2 minutes. Using a slotted spoon, transfer the livers to a plate; cover with aluminum foil to keep warm.

3) In the same skillet, heat the remaining 1 tablespoon oil over medium heat. Add the onion and cook, stirring often, until softened and translucent, 3 to 5 minutes. Add the fresh and soaked mushrooms and the remaining salt and pepper. Cook, stirring occasionally, until the mushrooms begin to brown, about 7 minutes.

4) Add the rice and stir for 1 minute. Add the remaining Marsala and reduce the heat to medium. Cook, stirring constantly, until the rice almost completely absorbs the liquid, about 1 minute. Add the mushroom-soaking liquid and cook until it is absorbed, about 3 minutes. Add 1 cup of the broth and stir constantly until the rice almost completely absorbs the broth, about 3 minutes. Continue adding the broth 1 cup at a time, stirring constantly, waiting until the broth is absorbed before adding more. At the end, the rice should be al dente and slightly creamy. (You may not use all of the broth by the time the rice is done.) Just before the rice is done, fold in the chicken livers to heat them through. Stir in the butter and sprinkle with the parsley. Serve at once, with a bowl of grated Parmesan cheese on the side.

Shrimp and Asparagus Risotto

*T*his is just the kind of risotto *you would get in a good Venetian trattoria. It is a wonderful dish to serve in celebration of spring asparagus. This dish calls for a couple of extra steps to extract every bit of the vegetable's flavor, but they're simple and worth the effort.*

Makes 4 to 6 servings

1 pound asparagus, tough ends snapped off and reserved
¾ pound large shrimp, peeled, deveined, and cut into ½-inch pieces, shells reserved
1 medium celery rib, coarsely chopped
1 garlic clove, unpeeled, crushed with a knife
1 sprig of parsley
1¼ teaspoons salt
2 tablespoons extra-virgin olive oil

¼ cup chopped shallots
1 tablespoon chopped parsley
2 teaspoons chopped fresh sage or ½ teaspoon crumbled dried
2 cups Arborio rice
½ cup dry white wine
3 tablespoons Cognac or brandy
⅛ teaspoon freshly ground pepper
1 tablespoon unsalted butter

1) In a heavy-bottomed Dutch oven, bring 8 cups water, the tough asparagus stalks (reserve the asparagus spears), the shrimp shells, celery, garlic, parsley sprig, and 1 teaspoon salt to a boil over high heat. Reduce the heat to low. Simmer until the stalks are very tender, about 30 minutes. Strain into a large bowl and discard the solids.

2) Return the asparagus/shrimp broth to the Dutch oven and bring to a boil over high heat. Add the asparagus spears and cook until barely tender, about 3 minutes. Strain into a bowl. Dry out the Dutch oven. Cut 1 inch off the top of each asparagus spear and set the tops aside. Coarsely chop the spears. Place the chopped spears with 1 cup of the broth in a blender and puree. Stir the puree into the broth, set aside, and keep hot.

3) In the same Dutch oven, heat the olive oil over medium heat. Add the shallots, chopped parsley, and sage. Cook, stirring often, until the shallots soften, about 2 minutes. Add the rice and stir for 1 minute. Add the wine, Cognac, the remaining ¼ teaspoon salt, and the pepper. Cook, stirring constantly, until the rice almost completely absorbs the liquid, about 2 minutes. Add 1 cup of the asparagus broth and reduce the heat to medium. Cook, stirring constantly, until the rice almost completely absorbs the broth, about 3 minutes. Continue adding the broth 1 cup at a time, stirring constantly, waiting until the broth is almost completely absorbed before adding more. When 2 cups of the broth remain, stir in the shrimp. At the end, the rice should be al dente and slightly creamy and the shrimp cooked through. (If necessary, add ½ cup hot water and cook longer until rice is done.) Stir in the butter. Serve immediately in warmed bowls, garnishing with the reserved asparagus tips.

Mediterranean Shrimp Risotto

Makes 4 to 6 servings

2 tablespoons extra-virgin olive oil
¾ pound medium shrimp, peeled
   and deveined
2 tablespoons butter
1 small onion, finely chopped
2 garlic cloves, minced
1½ cups Arborio rice
½ cup dry white wine
6 cups hot Fish Broth (page 26) or
   3 cups clam juice mixed with
   3 cups water

1 tablespoon tomato paste
1 medium red bell pepper,
   roasted, seeded, and diced, or
   ½ cup diced jarred roasted red
   peppers
1 cup thawed frozen peas
⅓ cup chopped fresh basil
1 tablespoon minced parsley
⅛ teaspoon freshly ground
   pepper
Salt

1) In a large skillet, heat 1 tablespoon of the olive oil over medium-high heat. Add the shrimp and cook, stirring occasionally, until they are curled and pink, 2 to 3 minutes. Transfer to a plate and set aside.

2) Heat 1 tablespoon of the butter and the remaining 1 tablespoon oil in the skillet over medium heat. Add the onion and garlic and cook, stirring often, until the onion is softened, 3 to 5 minutes. Add the rice and cook, stirring, for 2 to 3 minutes. Add the wine. Cook, stirring constantly, until the rice almost completely absorbs the wine, about 2 minutes.

3) In a medium bowl, blend the hot fish broth and tomato paste to dissolve the paste. Add 1 cup of the fish broth to the rice and reduce the heat to medium. Cook, stirring constantly, until the rice almost completely absorbs the broth, about 3 minutes. Continue to cook, adding the broth 1 cup at a time and stirring constantly, waiting until it is almost completely absorbed before adding more. When 1 cup broth remains, stir the cooked shrimp, red bell pepper, peas, basil, parsley, and ground pepper into the risotto. Continue adding broth as before. At the end, the rice should be al dente and slightly creamy. Stir in the remaining butter. Season with salt to taste. Serve immediately.

Rice Casserole with Pork, Zucchini, and Clams

This simple and very
*Mediterranean casserole is easy to make and deliciously tasty.
An added bonus is that it works very well with instant rice,
proving that tradition and time can go together.* **Makes 6 servings**

1 pound pork tenderloin, cut into
   1-inch cubes
2 tablespoons extra-virgin olive
   oil
1 (16-ounce) can tomato sauce
1 garlic clove
3 to 4 basil leaves

1 sprig parsley
Salt and freshly ground pepper
2 small zucchini, cut into 1-inch
   cubes
1½ cups instant rice
1 (6-ounce) can chopped clams

1) Preheat the oven to 400 degrees F.

2) Place the pork in a 14-inch-long oval baking dish from which you can
serve. Add the olive oil and toss; add the tomato sauce and toss again.

3) Chop together the garlic, basil, and parsley. Add to the casserole
and mix well. Season with salt and pepper. Cover tightly with aluminum foil
and bake 45 minutes. Add the zucchini, cover, and continue cooking
15 minutes longer, or until the pork is thoroughly cooked.

4) Combine the rice and the clams with their juices. Turn off the oven
and remove the casserole, add the rice mixture to the meat, and mix well.
Loosely cover the casserole and return it to the oven. Let it stand 5 minutes,
or until the rice is tender. Serve immediately.

Rice and Vegetable *Sartù*

Baked rice casseroles, like *this* sartù *and the French* tian, *are found throughout Mediterranean cooking. They offer a clever, tasty way to use the vegetables from yesterday's dinner. If you don't have a large flameproof baking dish, such as one of enameled cast-iron, use a 12-inch skillet with a heatproof handle.*   ***Makes 6 servings***

2 tablespoons extra-virgin olive oil
1 medium zucchini, cut into ½-inch cubes
1 cup converted rice
2¾ cups hot milk
1 cup chopped fresh spinach
4 tablespoons butter

¼ cup grated Parmesan cheese
1 hard-cooked egg, chopped
1 raw egg, beaten
½ teaspoon salt
⅛ teaspoon freshly ground pepper
2 cups shredded smoked mozzarella cheese

1) Preheat the oven to 375 degrees F. In a large (about 9 × 13 × 2-inch) flameproof baking dish, heat the olive oil over medium-high heat. Add the zucchini and cook, turning occasionally, until softened, 3 to 5 minutes. Using a slotted spoon, transfer to a plate and set aside.

2) Add the rice and 1 cup hot water. Bring to a boil and reduce heat to medium. Cook, stirring, until the rice absorbs the water, about 5 minutes. Add the milk, reduce the heat to medium-low, and cook, stirring often, until the milk is reduced to ¼ cup, 8 to 10 minutes. Remove from the heat.

3) Stir in the zucchini, spinach, 3 tablespoons of the butter, 2 tablespoons of the Parmesan cheese, the hard-cooked egg, the raw egg, salt, and pepper. Stir in 1 cup of the mozzarella. Smooth the top and sprinkle with the remaining 1 cup mozzarella and 2 tablespoons Parmesan. Dot with the remaining butter.

4) Bake until the cheese is melted and the top is golden brown, 30 to 40 minutes. Let stand for 10 minutes before serving.

Pizza and Savory Pies

I once wrote that pizza had conquered more of the world than the legions of Julius Caesar. Have you ever visited a country where there was no pizza? I have even encountered it in China. And why not?

There is something incredibly appealing about this round of crisp, warm, chewy dough topped with everything from tomatoes and cheese to sausages and vegetables. It is an incredibly tasty one-pot (or in this case "one-pan") food that can be enjoyed almost any hour of the day or night.

With store-bought pizza dough, or even frozen bread dough, you can make pizza in your own kitchen with very little effort. Frozen pizza dough, sold in supermarkets, produces excellent results if you defrost it at the bottom of your refrigerator for four hours or over-night. The dough is beautifully pliable and makes a crisp crust. Of course, I've included an easy food proc-essor recipe for making your own pizza dough at home, if you prefer. You just need to remember to allow an extra hour for the dough to rise before rolling it out.

Here you'll find a variety of pizzas, from the classic, impeccably simple Pizza Margherita, topped only with fresh tomatoes, basil, and mozzarella cheese, to Pizza Marinara, brimming with seafood, to a hearty Sunday Night Pizza, loaded with cheeses, sa-lami, and sauce. Traditional Italian-filled breads and several tortas, savory pies filled with meat, vegetables, and cheese, round out the chapter.

Homemade Pizza Dough

*T*he food processor makes short work of homemade pizza dough. This one can be refrigerated for up to 36 hours (just punch the dough whenever it rises to double its original size) or frozen for up to 2 months. To get the best results with rapid-rise yeast, follow the instructions on the packet. **Makes about 2 pounds**

1 (¼-ounce) envelope active dry yeast
½ teaspoon sugar
1 cup warm (100 to 110 degrees F.) water

3½ cups unbleached flour or bread flour
3 tablespoons extra-virgin olive oil
1½ teaspoons salt

1) In a small bowl, dissolve the yeast and sugar in ¼ cup of the warm water. Stir in 1 teaspoon of the flour. Let stand until it starts to bubble, about 10 minutes.

2) In a food processor, pulse the remaining flour, olive oil, and salt to combine. With the machine on, add the yeast mixture. Process, adding enough of the remaining warm water until the dough forms a ball on top of the blade. If this doesn't happen, add flour, 1 tablespoon at a time, and process until you have a firm ball. Transfer the dough to a lightly floured surface. Using floured hands, knead the dough until smooth and elastic, about 1 minute. (To make the dough by hand, prepare the yeast mixture. Place the flour, olive oil, and salt in a large bowl. Stir in the yeast mixture, adding more flour and water as needed to make a soft dough. Turn out onto a lightly floured work surface. Knead until the dough is soft and elastic, about 10 minutes.)

3) Gather up the dough into a ball. Place in a large, lightly oiled bowl; turn to coat with oil. With a sharp knife, cut a large, shallow "X" in the top. Cover with plastic wrap and drape a kitchen towel over the bowl. Let stand in a warm place until the dough has doubled in volume, about 1 hour. Punch down and knead briefly before using.

Pizza Margherita

*T*his is a pizza classic, designed in the late nineteenth century by a patriotic pizzaiolo (pizza baker) in honor of the Italian Queen Margherita. It features the colors of the Italian flag, red tomatoes, green basil, and white mozzarella.

Makes 4 servings

2 tablespoons extra-virgin olive oil
1 pound pizza or bread dough, thawed if frozen, at room temperature
4 ripe plum tomatoes, thinly sliced

2 tablespoons chopped fresh basil plus at least 12 whole basil leaves
1 pound mozzarella cheese, thinly sliced

1) Preheat the oven to 450 degrees F. Set the rack in the upper third of the oven. Lightly brush a 14-inch round pizza pan with some of the olive oil. Place the dough in the pan and stretch and pat out in a circle to cover the pan. If the dough feels sticky, lightly flour your hands. Brush the remaining oil over the surface of the dough.

2) Arrange the tomato slices over the dough, leaving a 1-inch border around the edges. Sprinkle with the chopped basil. Top with the mozzarella slices, but let the tomatoes peek out from under the cheese. Let stand in a warm place until the dough looks puffy, about 20 minutes.

3) Bake until the crust is well browned, about 20 minutes. Serve immediately, garnished with the whole basil leaves.

Pizza Marinara

*T*omatoes and seafood make
*this a succulent pizza that you won't find in your neighborhood
pizzeria (unless you happen to live in Palermo). This pizza gets a
two-step baking process—to be sure the fish doesn't get overcooked, the topping is added after the dough is almost done.*

Makes 4 servings

3 tablespoons extra-virgin olive
  oil
1 pound bread or pizza dough,
  homemade (page 145) or
  thawed, at room temperature
½ pound cooked shrimp or
  crabmeat

1 (6-ounce) can clams, drained
3 ripe plum tomatoes, peeled,
  seeded, and chopped
2 teaspoons chopped parsley
½ teaspoon dried basil
1 garlic clove, finely chopped
Freshly ground pepper

1) Position a rack in the bottom third of the oven and preheat to 450
degrees F. Set the rack in the upper third of the oven. Lightly brush a
14-inch round pizza pan with some of the olive oil. Place the dough in the
pan and stretch and pat it out in a circle to cover the pan. If the dough
feels sticky, lightly flour your hands. Let stand in a warm place until the
dough looks puffy, about 20 minutes. Bake until the dough is golden
brown, 15 to 20 minutes.

2) Meanwhile, mix all the remaining ingredients in a medium bowl.
Leaving a 1-inch border, spread the mixture over the top of the pizza.
Return to the oven and bake just until the topping is heated through, about
5 minutes. Cut into wedges to serve.

Pizza with Spinach, Pancetta, and Provolone

Fresh spinach makes this *pizza especially delicate. Pancetta is unsmoked Italian bacon, but the pork belly meat is rolled up into a thick log shape, and each slice is actually a spiraled bacon strip.* ***Makes 4 servings***

3½ tablespoons extra-virgin olive oil

1 pound bread or pizza dough, homemade (page 145) or thawed, at room temperature

1 pound fresh spinach leaves, well washed and dried

¼ pound shredded provolone cheese

2 (¼-inch-thick) slices pancetta, unrolled, or 4 strips bacon, cut lengthwise into 16 thin strips

2 tablespoons grated Parmesan cheese

Freshly ground pepper

1) Position a rack in the bottom third of the oven and preheat to 500 degrees F. Set the rack in the upper third of the oven. Lightly brush a 14-inch round pizza pan with olive oil. Place the dough in the pan and stretch and pat out in a circle to cover the pan. If the dough feels sticky, lightly flour your hands. Let stand in a warm place 15 minutes.

2) Discard the thick stems from the spinach. A few at a time, stack the leaves and cut into thin shreds. In a medium bowl, toss the spinach shreds with 2 tablespoons of the oil. Sprinkle the spinach over the dough, leaving a 1-inch border. Sprinkle with the provolone cheese. Arrange the pancetta strips in a lattice pattern over the top of the spinach. Sprinkle with the Parmesan cheese, then drizzle with the remaining oil. Season with freshly ground pepper to taste.

3) Bake until the edges are beginning to brown, about 15 minutes. Reduce the heat to 400 degrees F., then continue baking until the crust is well browned, about 10 minutes longer. Cut into wedges to serve.

Sunday Night Pizza

My mother often made this salami and cheese pizza for one of her light Sunday evening suppers. For easy eating, use an Italian salami with a small diameter, like the Italian cacciatorino; otherwise use Genoa salami cut into quarters. Serve it any night of the week for a delicious "one-pan" meal, Italian style. **Makes 4 servings**

1½ cups ricotta cheese

2 tablespoons extra-virgin olive oil

1 pound pizza or bread dough, thawed if frozen, at room temperature

¾ cup Marinara Sauce (recipe follows)

¼ cup grated Parmesan cheese

¼ teaspoon freshly ground pepper

¼ pound thinly sliced salami

¼ pound shredded mozzarella cheese

1) Position a rack in the bottom third of the oven and preheat to 450 degrees F. Spoon the ricotta into a coffee filter or fine sieve and let drain for at least 10 minutes to remove excess whey.

2) Meanwhile, lightly brush a 14-inch round pizza pan with some of the olive oil. Place the dough in the pan and stretch and pat it out in a circle to fit the pan. If the dough feels sticky, lightly flour your hands. Brush the remaining oil over the surface of the dough. Spread the marinara sauce over the dough, leaving a 1-inch margin.

3) In a medium bowl, mix the ricotta and Parmesan cheeses with the pepper. Spread the cheese mixture over the sauce. Top with the salami and sprinkle the mozzarella cheese over all. Cover loosely with plastic wrap. Let stand in a warm place until the dough looks puffy, about 20 minutes.

4) Bake until the crust is browned, about 20 minutes. Reduce the heat to 375 degrees F. and continue cooking until the underside of the crust is firm and well browned (lift with a spatula to check), 5 to 10 minutes.

Marinara Sauce

It would be a likely assumption that marinara sauce would have something to do with fish. Actually, it's named after the fishermen, as the sauce was a favorite on ships when a quickly prepared, zesty sauce was needed to dress pasta or turn into a fish stew.   ***Makes about 2 cups***

1 (16-ounce) can crushed
  tomatoes
2 tablespoons extra-virgin olive
  oil
2 garlic cloves, crushed through
  a press

1 teaspoon tomato paste
½ teaspoon dried oregano or
  basil
2 teaspoons chopped parsley
Salt and freshly ground pepper

1) Combine all of the ingredients except the salt and pepper in a medium saucepan and bring to a simmer over medium heat. Reduce the heat to low and cover.

2) Simmer, stirring often, until the sauce is slightly thickened, about 20 minutes. Season with salt and pepper to taste.

Calzone with Mortadella and Two Cheeses

*C*alzone *means "trouser leg," and although today's crescent-shaped turnover doesn't look like pants, the original version was a dough-wrapped salami or sausage and had an elongated shape.* ***Makes 4 servings***

1 cup ricotta, well drained
1 teaspoon chopped fresh basil
¼ teaspoon freshly ground
  pepper
2 pounds pizza or bread dough,
  thawed if frozen, at room
  temperature
1½ tablespoons extra-virgin
  olive oil

2 ripe plum tomatoes, coarsely
  chopped
2 cups shredded mozzarella
  cheese
¼ pound sliced mortadella, cut
  into ¼-inch-wide strips

1) Preheat the oven to 400 degrees F. Set the racks in the upper third and center of the oven. In a medium bowl, mix the ricotta, basil, and pepper.

2) Cut the dough into 4 equal portions. Working with 1 piece of dough at a time, roll each out on a lightly floured surface into a 9-inch round. Brush each round lightly with olive oil. Spoon about ¼ cup of the ricotta mixture on the lower half of each circle, leaving a 1-inch border around the edges. Top each with one-fourth of the chopped tomato. Sprinkle each with ½ cup mozzarella cheese and one-fourth of the mortadella. Fold each circle in half to enclose the filling and press the edges firmly with a fork to seal. Place on 2 lightly oiled large baking sheets. Let stand 10 minutes at room temperature.

3) Place the calzoni in the oven and reduce the oven temperature to 375 degrees. Bake until the tops are golden brown, 25 to 30 minutes. Halfway through baking, switch the positions of the baking sheets from top to bottom. Serve hot.

Prosciutto and Mozzarella Pizza Bread

In the charming Abruzzo town of Sulmona, the Monastery of Santa Chiara's is famous for this flat potato bread studded with prosciutto and mozzarella. The potatoes keep the dough light and tender. Similar to focaccia, this bread is substantial enough to be a main course, served with a crisp tossed salad.

Makes 4 servings

1 large baking potato (about 8 ounces)
1 (¼-ounce) packet active dry yeast
¼ cup warm (100 to 110 degrees F.) water
2 cups unbleached all-purpose flour
2 tablespoons butter, softened
2 eggs
¼ teaspoon freshly ground pepper
¾ teaspoon salt
¼ pound thickly sliced prosciutto, cut into ¼-inch dice
¼ pound smoked mozzarella cheese, cut into ¼-inch dice
2 teaspoons extra-virgin olive oil

1) In a medium saucepan of lightly salted water, cook the potato over high heat until tender, about 20 minutes. Drain and cool. Peel and mash the potato.

2) In a small bowl, dissolve the yeast in the warm water. Let stand until it bubbles, about 5 minutes. Stir in 2 tablespoons of the flour until smooth. Cover with plastic wrap. Let stand in a warm place for 1 hour. Set aside.

3) In a food processor, pulse 1½ cups of the flour, the mashed potato, and the butter until the mixture resembles coarse meal. With the machine on, add the eggs, yeast mixture, salt, and pepper. Process until the dough forms a ball on top of the blade. If the dough is too wet, add a little more flour, 1 tablespoon at a time. If the dough is crumbly and dry, add additional water, 1 tablespoon at a time, and follow the same procedure. Process the ball of dough to knead for 45 seconds.

4) Transfer to a lightly floured surface. Using floured hands, gradually knead in the prosciutto and mozzarella. (To make the dough by hand, place the flour, mashed potato, and butter in a large bowl. Using a pastry blender, cut the ingredients together until they resemble coarse meal. Stir in the yeast mixture, adding more flour as needed to make a soft dough. Turn out onto a lightly floured work surface. Knead until the dough is soft and elastic, about 10 minutes. Knead in the mozzarella and prosciutto.) Cover the dough with plastic wrap and let stand for 1 hour.

5) Brush a 10-inch round baking dish with the olive oil. Stretch and pat the dough into the dish. Cover with plastic wrap. Let stand in a warm place 10 to 15 minutes.

6) Preheat the oven to 375 degrees F. Bake the bread until the top is nicely browned, 30 to 40 minutes. Serve hot or at room temperature.

Naked Pizza Rustica

True *pizza rustica is a deep-dish, double-crust pizza usually filled with a cheesy ricotta and spinach combination. One day, I had all the ingredients, but I didn't feel like making the dough. So, I improvised baking the pizza "naked," without the dough, and what a success! It is the perfect lunch or brunch dish, served with a refreshing tomato and cucumber salad, or cooled to room temperature and cut into little squares to pass with drinks.* ***Makes 4 servings***

1 tablespoon butter, softened
¼ cup dried bread crumbs
4 eggs
3 pounds ricotta, well drained
½ pound sliced salami, preferably soppressata, very finely chopped

1 (10-ounce) package frozen chopped spinach, thawed and squeezed to remove excess moisture
½ cup grated Parmesan cheese
¼ teaspoon freshly ground pepper

1) Preheat the oven to 375 degrees F. Coat the inside of a 10-inch deep-dish pie plate with the butter. Sprinkle with 2 tablespoons of the bread crumbs, tilt to coat the plate, and tap out the excess crumbs.

2) In a medium bowl, beat the eggs with the remaining 2 tablespoons bread crumbs. Add the ricotta, salami, spinach, Parmesan cheese, and pepper and mix well. Pour into the pie plate and smooth the top.

3) Bake until a toothpick inserted in the center comes out clean, about 45 minutes. Cool for 10 minutes before slicing. Serve hot or at room temperature.

Salmon Pie with Marsala and Smoked Mozzarella

*T*his sports a golden brown filo
crust enclosing a salmon and smoked mozzarella filling. While
I make it most often with cooked salmon, other leftover fish can be
substituted. These pies are a bonus for a busy cook.

Makes 4 to 6 servings

4 eggs
2 cups cooked, flaked salmon
1 cup shredded smoked
    mozzarella or smoked Edam
    cheese
3 scallions, finely chopped
1 tablespoon chopped parsley

1 tablespoon dry Marsala wine
¼ teaspoon salt
⅛ teaspoon freshly ground
    pepper
4 tablespoons butter, melted
6 sheets of filo dough, thawed if
    frozen

1) In a medium bowl, beat the eggs. Add the salmon, smoked mozzarella
cheese, scallions, parsley, Marsala, salt, and pepper. Mix well.

2) Brush a 10-inch deep-dish pie plate with some of the melted butter.
Fold 1 filo dough sheet in half vertically. Center in the pie plate, letting
the dough hang over the edges. Brush with melted butter. Repeat with 2 more
sheets of folded filo dough, with each hanging over a different part of the
edge, so the bottom and sides of the pie plate are completely covered. Brush
each with butter. (Do not worry if the filo dough sheets break or crack.)
Spread the salmon mixture in the plate. Top with the remaining 3 filo dough
sheets, folding each in half vertically and brushing each sheet with
butter, including the top sheet. Tuck the edges of the filo dough inside of the
pie plate. If desired, the recipe can be made ahead to this point and
refrigerated for up to 3 hours.

3) Place in a cold oven and turn the temperature to 350 degrees F. Bake
until the pie is golden brown, 30 to 35 minutes (allow 5 to 10 minutes
longer if the pie is cold). Cool for 10 minutes before slicing. Serve while hot.

Veal and Eggplant Torta

Ground veal, prosciutto, and an assortment of vegetables combine to make a hearty filling for a puff pastry crust. Frozen puff pastry is a versatile ingredient to have on hand, but it works best when defrosted overnight in the refrigerator. For best flavor, look for prepared puff pastry made with butter rather than vegetable shortening or margarine.

Makes 4 to 6 servings

¼ cup extra-virgin olive oil
1 small onion, chopped
½ pound ground veal or turkey
2 tablespoons dry Marsala wine
½ teaspoon salt
¼ teaspoon freshly ground pepper
1 medium eggplant (1 pound), cut into ½-inch dice
¼ pound green beans, cut into ¼-inch lengths
1 cup canned peeled tomatoes, drained and chopped

1 teaspoon dried oregano
1 cup fresh or frozen peas
¼ pound thickly sliced prosciutto, finely chopped
1 egg, beaten
2 tablespoons dried bread crumbs
1 (17¼-ounce) package frozen puff pastry sheets, thawed
1 tablespoon butter, melted

1) In a 10-inch cast-iron skillet, heat 2 tablespoons of the olive oil over medium heat. Add the onion and cook, stirring often, until softened and translucent, 3 to 5 minutes. Add the veal and cook, stirring often, until the veal is lightly browned, about 6 minutes. Add the Marsala and cook until it evaporates, about 1 minute. Season with the salt and pepper. Transfer to a medium bowl.

2) Add the remaining 2 tablespoons oil to the skillet and heat over medium-high heat. Add the eggplant and green beans. Cook, stirring occasionally, until the vegetables are softened, adding more oil to the skillet if needed as the vegetables cook, about 10 minutes. Add the tomatoes and oregano and bring to a simmer. Reduce the heat to medium-low and cook until the tomato juices are slightly thickened, about 10 minutes. Stir in the peas and prosciutto. Transfer to the bowl with the veal. Cool slightly, then stir in the egg and bread crumbs. Cool completely. Rinse and dry the skillet.

3) Preheat the oven to 375 degrees F. Lightly oil the same skillet. Stretch 1 sheet of puff pastry to fit the skillet, letting the excess dough hang over the edges. Fill with the cooled veal mixture. Stretch the other puff pastry sheet on top, stretching the pastry as needed to cover the filling. Press the 2 sheets of dough together to seal, then trim excess dough. Cut a small hole in the center to allow steam to escape. Brush the dough with the melted butter. Place on a baking sheet.

4) Bake until the top is golden brown, 30 to 40 minutes. Cool for 10 minutes before slicing.

Savory Pumpkin Pie

*T**his is not the typical Thanksgiving pumpkin pie, but a savory, free-form torta from Abruzzo. It is a favorite winter dish with the Abruzzesi; they make it with zucca, a firm winter squash. Canned pumpkin works just as well, but be sure not to use the seasoned pumpkin pie mix.*

Makes 6 to 8 servings

2 tablespoons butter, melted
1½ cups canned pumpkin
1 (10-ounce) package frozen chopped spinach, thawed and squeezed to remove excess moisture
¼ pound sliced mortadella or boiled ham, cut into ¼-inch dice
¼ cup shredded Parmesan cheese

¼ cup chopped walnuts
1 egg, beaten
1 tablespoon flour
½ teaspoon grated nutmeg
¼ teaspoon salt
⅛ teaspoon freshly ground pepper
1 (17¼-ounce) package frozen puff pastry sheets, thawed

1) Preheat the oven to 400 degrees F. In a medium bowl, combine 1 tablespoon of the melted butter with all of the remaining ingredients except the puff pastry. Mix to blend well.

2) Place 1 puff pastry sheet on a lightly buttered baking sheet. Spread the pumpkin mixture over the pastry, leaving a 1-inch border around the edges. Top with the other sheet and press the edges with a fork to seal. Brush the top of the pie with the remaining 1 tablespoon butter.

3) Bake 30 to 40 minutes, until the top is golden brown. Cool for 10 minutes before slicing.

Zucchini Cheese Pie with Filo Crust

Golden, flaky, buttery filo dough encloses a mouthwatering filling with zucchini, mortadella, and three cheeses. It is an excellent choice for a picnic, since it is just as good at room temperature as it is served hot.

Makes 6 to 8 servings

About ⅓ cup extra-virgin olive oil
1 large red onion, thinly sliced
4 medium zucchini, cut into
  ¼-inch rounds (about
  1¼ pounds)
¼ pound mortadella, cut into
  thin strips
¼ cup grated Parmesan cheese

1 tablespoon chopped parsley
12 sheets filo dough, thawed if
  frozen
½ pound mozzarella cheese,
  thinly sliced
¼ pound Swiss cheese, finely
  chopped, or additional
  mozzarella

1) In a 10-inch ovenproof skillet, heat 2 tablespoons of the olive oil over medium heat. Add the onion and cook, stirring often, until softened and translucent, about 5 minutes. Add the zucchini and cook, tossing, until barely tender, about 5 minutes. Do not overcook. Transfer to a bowl. Stir in the mortadella, Parmesan cheese, and parsley. Cool completely.

2) Preheat the oven to 350 degrees F. Lightly oil a 13 × 9-inch baking pan. Layer 6 filo dough sheets in the pan, letting the dough hang over the edge and brushing each sheet lightly with half of the remaining oil. Spread half the zucchini mixture in the pan. Top with the mozzarella cheese. Spread with the remaining zucchini mixture and sprinkle with the Swiss cheese. Layer the 6 remaining filo dough sheets on top, lightly brushing each sheet with most of the remaining oil. Tuck the ends of the filo dough inside the pan. Brush the top of the dough with oil.

3) Bake about 30 minutes, until the pie is golden brown. Cool for 5 minutes before serving.

Italian Verdura

It is said that we Italians have a special way with vegetables. Part of this supposed genius must be attributed to the warm, sunny climate of the Mediterranean, which produces such a bounty of tomatoes, eggplant, zucchini, artichokes, broccoli, beans, cabbages, and squash, as well as the fresh herbs and good extra-virgin olive oil to accompany them. Part of it is the simple and tasty ways we have invented to turn this excellent produce into a meal.

For me, *verdura,* or vegetables, are the crowning touch to any meal. In Italy, main dishes of meat or chicken are always served with a green vegetable as accompaniment: spinach, Swiss chard, escarole, or broccoli di rape, for example. But since we Italians love vegetables so much, quite often they are served in combination as a main course. They can be baked with eggs in a flan, or stuffed with other vegetables, cheeses, sausages, and bread crumbs. They are braised, baked, grilled, and broiled. In fact, for years it was almost a ritual to have a casserole made of vegetables for supper at night on a day when we had eaten a large meal with meat for lunch. Perhaps we Italians have an innate sense of good nutrition.

While all the recipes in this chapter were designed as vegetable main courses, if you are not used to vegetarian eating, you might like to accompany some with a wedge of cheese, a bit of salami or prosciutto, or a hard-cooked egg. Many of them, such as the Roman Artichokes with Potatoes, Eggplant Sorrento Style, and Zucchini Stuffed with Walnuts and Cheese, would work well in smaller portions as a starter or as a side dish in an American-style meal.

Roman Artichokes
with Potatoes

Braised stuffed artichokes are *a Roman classic. My mother liked to throw some potato into the pot to turn this savory dish into a one-pot supper.*

Makes 6 servings

2 lemons, halved
6 large artichokes, stems attached if possible
½ cup bread crumbs
6 tablespoons extra-virgin olive oil
¼ cup chopped fresh mint, plus 2 sprigs of mint
1 tablespoon finely chopped parsley, plus 2 sprigs of parsley

3 garlic cloves—1 minced and 2 crushed under a knife
⅛ teaspoon grated nutmeg
¼ teaspoon salt
⅛ teaspoon freshly ground pepper
6 small red potatoes, scrubbed and quartered

1) Squeeze the juice of 1 lemon into a large bowl and add 4 cups cold water. Prepare 1 artichoke at a time, rubbing the cut areas with the remaining lemon halves as you work. Cut off the artichoke stem at the base. Using a small sharp knife, pare away the dark green skin. Drop the stem into the lemon water. Bend back and break off the tough dark green artichoke leaves until the pale green center leaves are revealed. Cut off the top 1 inch of the artichoke. Spread open the leaves to reveal the choke in the center. Pull out the prickly choke leaves. Using the tip of a teaspoon, scrape out the hairy choke and discard. Drop the trimmed artichokes into the lemon water as they are ready.

2) In a medium bowl, combine the bread crumbs, ¼ cup of the olive oil, the chopped mint and parsley, minced garlic, nutmeg, salt, and pepper. Stuff the artichokes with the crumb mixture. Arrange the artichokes snugly in a large Dutch oven. Insert the potatoes, artichoke stems, mint and parsley sprigs, and crushed garlic among the artichokes. Pour in 1½ cups of the lemon water. Drizzle the tops of the artichokes with the remaining 2 tablespoons oil.

3) Bring to a boil over high heat. Reduce the heat to low, cover, and cook until the artichokes are tender and the sauce has thickened, about 40 minutes. Transfer each artichoke with some potatoes and the stem to a soup bowl and add some of the potatoes. Discard the crushed garlic and herb sprigs, and pour some sauce over each artichoke.

VARIATION: The bread stuffing can be replaced with a cheese stuffing. In a medium bowl, mix 1¼ cups ricotta cheese, 2 ounces chopped prosciutto or salami, and 2 tablespoons grated Parmesan cheese. During the last 10 minutes of cooking, top each artichoke with a slice of mozzarella cheese.

Artichoke and Vegetable Flan

*L*eftover vegetables never go to waste in the Italian kitchen, and this colorful custard is a good example of how a little thrift can provide a fine dividend. I always start with artichokes—in the best circumstances, I would use fresh spring baby artichokes, but frozen artichoke hearts are always available and quite good. From there, it's up to you.

Makes 4 to 6 servings

¼ cup extra-virgin olive oil
1 (9-ounce) package frozen
  artichoke hearts, thawed
1½ cups chopped cooked
  vegetables, such as zucchini,
  broccoli, carrots, green beans,
  or corn, in any combination

3 large eggs, beaten
2 tablespoons all-purpose flour
¼ teaspoon grated nutmeg
½ teaspoon salt
⅛ teaspoon freshly ground
  pepper
¼ cup milk

1) Preheat the oven to 400 degrees F. In a 10-inch cast-iron skillet with ovenproof handle, heat 2 tablespoons of the olive oil over medium heat. Add the artichoke hearts. Cook, stirring often, until heated through, about 3 minutes. Add the vegetables and cook, stirring often, until all the vegetables are heated through, about 3 minutes. Transfer to a large bowl and cool. Wipe out the skillet with paper towels.

2) In a mixing bowl, beat the eggs with the flour, nutmeg, salt, and pepper until smooth. Mix in the milk. Stir in the vegetables.

3) In the skillet, heat the remaining 2 tablespoons oil over medium heat. Add the egg mixture. As the edges set, lift them up with a spatula and tilt the pan so the uncooked eggs flow underneath the cooked portion. Continue cooking until set but the top is still shiny, about 3 minutes.

4) Bake until the top is golden brown, 5 to 10 minutes. Serve immediately.

Confetti Frittata

*T*he little flecks of orange,
green, and red vegetables give this dish its name. Frittatas are
among my favorite ways to make a quick, nourishing meal.

Makes 4 to 6 servings

5 eggs
1 tablespoon grated Parmesan
  cheese
¼ teaspoon salt
¼ teaspoon freshly ground
  pepper
3 tablespoons extra-virgin olive
  oil

1 medium carrot, finely diced
1 ripe large tomato, seeded and
  cut into ½-inch cubes
2 cups loosely packed chopped
  fresh spinach leaves

1) In a medium bowl, whisk the eggs, cheese, salt and pepper. Set aside.

2) In a 10-inch skillet, preferably nonstick, heat 1 tablespoon of the olive
oil over medium heat. Add the carrots and cover. Cook, stirring often,
until the carrots are tender and lightly browned, 8 to 10 minutes. Add the
tomato cubes. Cook, uncovered, stirring often, until the juices evaporate,
about 6 minutes. Add the spinach and cook, stirring often, until wilted, about
3 minutes. Let cool for about 5 minutes, then add to the egg mixture in
the bowl.

3) Heat the remaining 2 tablespoons oil in the skillet over medium heat.
Pour the egg mixture into the skillet and mix gently. As the edges of the
frittata set, lift them up with a spatula and tilt the pan so the uncooked eggs
flow underneath the cooked portion. Continue cooking until the frittata
is set but the top is still shiny, about 3 minutes. Place a flat skillet lid or plate
over the frittata. Invert the skillet and plate together so the frittata falls
out onto the plate. Slide the frittata, cooked side up, back into the skillet.
Continue cooking until the underside is lightly browned, 3 to 5 minutes.
Transfer the frittata to a warmed round platter. Serve immediately.

Eggplant Sorrento Style

Eggplant, tomato, and mozzarella are a beloved trio throughout the Gulf of Naples. You need an equal number of eggplant slices, tomato rounds, mozzarella slices, and basil leaves to prepare this easy recipe. Most versions call for frying the eggplant in olive oil before assembling the dish. The eggplant guzzles up the oil, making the dish too oily, so I bake the eggplant, which takes care of the problem.

Makes 6 to 8 servings

2 medium-large eggplants
(about 2 pounds total),
sliced about ¼ inch thick
¼ cup extra-virgin olive oil
½ teaspoon salt
¼ teaspoon freshly ground
pepper

4 ripe medium tomatoes, sliced
about ¼ inch thick
1 pound mozzarella cheese,
thinly sliced
24 large basil leaves

1) Preheat the oven to 375 degrees F. Place the eggplant slices on lightly oiled baking sheets. Brush both sides with olive oil. Bake until the eggplant is softened, about 10 minutes. Turn and bake until almost tender throughout, about 5 minutes longer.

2) Remove from the oven. Season the eggplant slices with the salt and pepper. Top each with 1 tomato slice, 1 mozzarella slice, and 1 basil leaf. Return to the oven and bake until the cheese melts, about 10 minutes. Serve immediately.

Married Potatoes

In my birthplace, Abruzzo, *"married" mate with mozzarella cheese and ham in a truly savory way. It's a dish that represents the best of good country cooking. I remember that vineyard workers made this dish to eat cold in the fields for their midday break. I serve it hot more often than not, but it is delicious either way.* **Makes 6 servings**

3 large Idaho baking potatoes
  (about 1½ pounds), peeled
  and very thinly sliced
½ teaspoon salt
¼ teaspoon freshly ground
  pepper
2 tablespoons extra-virgin olive
  oil

1 pound mozzarella cheese,
  thinly sliced
½ pound smoked ham, coarsely
  chopped
2 tablespoons dried bread
  crumbs

1) Preheat the oven to 375 degrees F. Place half of the potatoes in a lightly oiled 10-inch round shallow baking dish. Season with ¼ teaspoon salt and ⅛ teaspoon pepper. Drizzle with 1 tablespoon of the olive oil. Cover with overlapping slices of the mozzarella cheese, then top with the ham. Cover with the remaining potatoes and season with the remaining ¼ teaspoon salt and ⅛ teaspoon pepper. Sprinkle with the bread crumbs and drizzle with the remaining 1 tablespoon oil. Cover with aluminum foil.

2) Bake for 30 minutes. Uncover and bake 30 minutes longer, until the potatoes are tender and the top is golden brown. Cool 15 minutes before serving.

Braised Potatoes and Green Beans

*T*his savory, rustic dish is very *popular with my vegetarian friends.*   ***Makes 4 to 6 servings***

¼ cup extra-virgin olive oil
10 medium red potatoes
  (2 pounds), peeled and sliced
½ pound green beans, preferably
  Italian broad beans, cut into
  1-inch lengths
1 large red onion, thinly sliced

1 garlic clove, minced
1 tablespoon chopped parsley
¼ teaspoon salt
¼ teaspoon freshly ground
  pepper
1½ cups vegetable or chicken
  broth, or more as needed

1) In a large, heavy-bottomed skillet, heat the olive oil over medium heat. Add the potatoes. Cook, turning occasionally, until lightly browned, about 8 minutes. Add the green beans, onion, and garlic. Cook, stirring often, until the onion softens, about 5 minutes. Stir in 1½ teaspoons of the parsley, the salt, and pepper. Pour in enough broth to barely cover the vegetables. Cover tightly and reduce the heat to medium-low.

2) Cook for 30 to 40 minutes, until the liquid is almost completely absorbed. Sprinkle with the remaining 1½ teaspoons parsley and serve immediately.

Herb-Stuffed Peppers with Mozzarella, Tomatoes, and Potatoes

Makes 6 servings

6 medium bell peppers, either
  green, red, or yellow, or a
  combination
1½ cups bread crumbs
3 anchovy fillets packed in oil,
  drained and finely minced, or
  1½ teaspoons anchovy paste
1 tablespoon chopped fresh basil
  or 1 teaspoon dried
1 teaspoon chopped fresh sage
  or ½ teaspoon dried
1 teaspoon chopped parsley
2 garlic cloves, minced
1 ripe large tomato, cut into
  6 rounds

3 ounces mozzarella cheese, cut
  into 6 slices
2 tablespoons extra-virgin olive
  oil
3 large Idaho baking potatoes
  (about 1½ pounds), peeled
  and cut into 8 wedges each
1 tablespoon chopped fresh
  rosemary or 1 teaspoon dried
¼ teaspoon salt
¼ teaspoon freshly ground
  pepper

1) Preheat the oven to 375 degrees F. Lightly oil a large roasting pan. Cut the tops off the peppers and set aside, discarding the stems. Scoop out and discard the seeds and ribs.

2) In a medium bowl, combine the bread crumbs, anchovies, basil, sage, parsley, and garlic. Insert 1 tomato slice and 1 mozzarella cheese slice inside each pepper. Stuff the peppers with the bread crumb mixture. Cover the peppers with their tops. Place in the roasting pan and drizzle with 1 tablespoon of the olive oil. Toss the potatoes with the remaining 1 tablespoon oil, the rosemary, salt, and pepper. Surround the peppers with the potatoes.

3) Bake 1 hour, or until the potatoes are soft. Serve hot or at room temperature.

Red Peppers with Sausage and Fava Bean Stuffing

I*talians love to stuff vegetables. Here red bell peppers are stuffed with a sausage filling and surrounded by fava beans to make a pretty color contrast. Fava beans are one of spring's culinary treats, and can be found at produce stores and supermarkets that have a Mediterranean clientele. You may substitute 2 cups frozen baby lima beans (added during the last 15 minutes of baking) or trimmed green beans.* **Makes 6 servings**

6 medium red bell peppers
¾ pound sweet Italian sausage, casings removed
1 egg, beaten
2 tablespoons dried bread crumbs
1 tablespoon grated Romano cheese
1 tablespoon chopped parsley

1½ cups beef broth
2 pounds fresh fava beans, shelled, or ½ pound green beans, cut into ½-inch lengths
1 teaspoon dried oregano
¼ teaspoon salt
⅛ teaspoon freshly ground pepper

1) Preheat the oven to 350 degrees F. Cut the tops off the peppers and discard. Scoop out and discard the seeds and ribs.

2) In a medium bowl, combine the sausage, egg, bread crumbs, cheese, and parsley. Loosely stuff the peppers with the sausage mixture. Place in a large round casserole. (If the peppers won't stand up, trim a tiny bit from the bottoms to stabilize them.) Pour the broth into the casserole.

3) Bake, basting occasionally, for 20 minutes. Scatter the beans around the peppers and season with the oregano, salt, and pepper. Bake until the peppers are tender and the sausage cooked through, 15 to 20 minutes longer. Serve hot.

Acorn Squash with Mortadella Stuffing

Acorn squash is another *vegetable that was created to be stuffed. That old friend of Italian cooks, mortadella, makes another appearance in this bread crumb stuffing. When you purchase mortadella for cooking, be sure the delicatessen slices it in one thick piece, then chop it as required at home. Otherwise, it will probably be cut into thin slices for sandwiches, and you won't get as much flavor in each bite.*

Makes 6 servings

3 acorn squash, halved
  horizontally, stems and
  seeds discarded
½ pound mortadella in 1 piece,
  coarsely chopped
1 cup bread crumbs
¼ cup grated Parmesan cheese
3 tablespoons extra-virgin olive
  oil

1 tablespoon chopped parsley
¼ teaspoon grated nutmeg
¼ teaspoon salt
¼ teaspoon freshly ground
  pepper
2 ounces sliced Jarlsberg cheese,
  finely chopped

1) Preheat the oven to 350 degrees F. Lightly oil a large rectangular baking dish. Place the squash in the dish, cut sides up. Add ½ cup water to the dish and bake until the squash are almost tender, about 20 minutes. Leave the oven on.

2) In a medium bowl, combine the mortadella, bread crumbs, Parmesan, 2 tablespoons of the olive oil, the parsley, nutmeg, salt, and pepper. Stuff the squash with the crumb mixture. Sprinkle with the Jarlsberg cheese. Drizzle the tops with the remaining 1 tablespoon oil.

3) Bake until the topping is browned and the cheese melts, 20 to 25 minutes. Serve immediately.

Vegetable Casserole alla Babi

Babi is a dear Italian friend of mine who lives with her husband and son in the charming city of Este, near Padua. This substantial casserole of potatoes, onions, eggplant, zucchini, and tomato is the kind of dish that many fine Italian cooks prepare for a light vegetarian meal, but hers is outstanding.

Makes 6 to 8 servings

6 tablespoons dried bread crumbs
2 tablespoons chopped parsley
2 teaspoons chopped fresh rosemary or 1 teaspoon dried
½ teaspoon salt
¼ teaspoon freshly ground pepper
2 large baking potatoes, peeled and cut into ¼-inch-thick rounds

2 large onions, thinly sliced
2 cups tomato puree
2 medium eggplants (about 2 pounds), cut into ¼-inch-thick rounds
4 medium zucchini (about 2 pounds), cut into ¼-inch-thick rounds
3 tablespoons extra-virgin olive oil

1) Preheat the oven to 375 degrees F. In a small bowl, mix 3 tablespoons of the bread crumbs, the parsley, rosemary, salt, and pepper.

2) Place half of the potatoes, overlapping as needed, in a lightly oiled 9 × 13-inch baking dish and top with a third of the onions. Sprinkle with a third of the bread crumb mixture and spread with a third of the tomato puree. Top with a layer of overlapping eggplant slices, then half of the remaining onions. Sprinkle with half of the remaining bread crumb mixture and spread with half of the remaining tomato puree. Top with a layer of overlapping zucchini and then the remaining onions, bread crumb mixture, and tomato puree. Finish with a layer of potatoes. Sprinkle with the plain bread crumbs and drizzle with the olive oil. Cover with aluminum foil.

3) Bake for 45 minutes. Uncover and bake until the vegetables are tender and the top is browned, about 15 minutes longer. Cool for 10 minutes before serving.

Zucchini Stuffed with Walnuts and Cheese

*T*hese stuffed zucchini are *cooked with white wine, which gives them a sophisticated touch. It is important to choose small zucchini for this dish—no longer than 7 inches. They make a nice light supper, served with a glass of the same wine used for the vegetables, and a dessert of cappuccino and biscotti.* **Makes 6 servings**

12 small zucchini (about
  2 pounds)
8 ounces mozzarella cheese, cut
  into ¼-inch cubes
1 cup bread crumbs
½ cup chopped walnuts
⅓ cup milk

1 tablespoon chopped parsley
¼ teaspoon salt
⅛ teaspoon freshly ground
  pepper
1 tablespoon extra-virgin olive
  oil
½ cup dry white wine

1) Preheat the oven to 375 degrees F. Lightly oil a large rectangular baking dish.

2) Cut each zucchini in half lengthwise. Using the tip of a spoon, scoop out the insides of the zucchini, leaving ½-inch-thick shells. Coarsely chop the zucchini flesh and place in a medium bowl. Add the mozzarella cheese, bread crumbs, walnuts, milk, parsley, salt, and pepper. Stuff the zucchini with the mixture. Place in the baking dish and drizzle with the olive oil. Pour the wine around the zucchini.

3) Bake, basting occasionally, 30 to 45 minutes, or until the zucchini are tender.

Zucchini, Tomato, and Mozzarella Gratin

Y*ou need fresh, ripe plum tomatoes for this vegetarian casserole—the large beefsteak variety may give off too much juice. For variety, mix ¼ pound chopped mortadella with the mozzarella cheese.*

Makes 6 servings

6 medium zucchini, cut into
 ¼-inch-thick rounds
1 pound ripe plum tomatoes,
 thinly sliced
3 tablespoons extra-virgin olive
 oil

½ teaspoon dried oregano
½ teaspoon salt
¼ teaspoon freshly ground
 pepper
½ pound mozzarella cheese, cut
 into ½-inch dice

1) Preheat the oven to 400 degrees F. Spread the zucchini slices in an even layer in a lightly oiled large rectangular baking dish. Insert about half of the tomato slices between the zucchini, evenly spacing the tomatoes throughout the dish.

2) Drizzle with 1 tablespoon of the olive oil and sprinkle with ¼ teaspoon oregano, ¼ teaspoon salt, and ⅛ teaspoon pepper. Cover with half the mozzarella cheese. Arrange the remaining tomatoes over the mozzarella. Drizzle with the remaining 2 tablespoons oil, ¼ teaspoon oregano, ¼ teaspoon salt, and ⅛ teaspoon pepper. Top with the remaining mozzarella.

3) Bake until the zucchini is tender, 30 to 35 minutes. Serve immediately.

Sardinian Zucchini and Tomato Casserole

The remote location of the island of Sardinia, off the western coast of Italy in the Mediterranean, allowed it to develop its own cuisine. One of its specialties is the semi-hard sheep's cheese called Pecorino Sardo, which adds its pleasant sharpness to this stovetop casserole. Use the fresh Pecorino Sardo with a dark yellow rind, rather than the aged, dried cheese with a black rind, which is better grated and used like Parmesan. Fresh Pecorino can be found at Italian grocers' and specialty cheese shops, or substitute grated Pecorino Romano cheese. **Makes 4 to 6 servings**

¼ cup extra-virgin olive oil
1 large onion, chopped
2 ripe large tomatoes, peeled, seeded, and cut into ½-inch cubes
4 large zucchini (1½ pounds), cut into ½-inch cubes
1 tablespoon chopped parsley

¾ pound fresh Pecorino Sardo cheese, cut into ½-inch cubes, or 1 cup grated Pecorino Romano cheese
¼ cup chopped basil
4 ounces mozzarella cheese, thinly sliced

1) In a large flameproof casserole or skillet, heat the olive oil over medium heat. Add the onion. Cook, stirring often, until the onion is softened and translucent, 3 to 5 minutes. Add the tomatoes and reduce the heat to medium-low. Cook, stirring often, until they give off their juices, about 10 minutes. Stir in the zucchini and parsley and cover. Cook until the zucchini are tender, 5 to 8 minutes.

2) Stir in the Pecorino cheese and the basil. Top with the sliced mozzarella. Cover and simmer until the mozzarella is melted, 5 to 8 minutes. Serve hot.

Mama's Poached Eggs in Tomato and Bell Pepper Sauce

This is another one of those *wonderful Sunday night meals that fills me with nostalgia every time I make it. Enjoy it the way my mother taught me—tear off a piece of bread from a crusty loaf to dip into the egg and sauce. Delizioso!*

Makes 6 servings

2 tablespoons extra-virgin olive oil

2 garlic cloves, peeled and crushed under a knife

2 medium green bell peppers, seeds and ribs discarded, cut into ½-inch-wide strips

1 (16-ounce) can peeled tomatoes, drained and coarsely chopped

½ teaspoon dried oregano

¼ teaspoon salt

¼ teaspoon freshly ground pepper

6 eggs

1) In a large skillet over medium heat, heat the olive oil. Add the garlic and cook until it begins to brown, about 1 minute. Add the bell peppers. Cook, stirring often, until the peppers are softened and beginning to brown, about 10 minutes. Add the tomatoes, oregano, salt, and pepper. Reduce the heat to medium-low. Cover and simmer until the sauce is thickened, about 15 minutes. Pick out and discard the garlic.

2) Working directly over the skillet, break an egg into the simmering sauce. Repeat with the remaining eggs, placing them in a circular pattern with the last egg in the center. Cook, covered, occasionally spooning the sauce over the eggs, until the eggs are set but the yolks are still runny, about 15 minutes. Serve directly from the skillet.

Index